Grade 4

MW00719122

COUNTDOWN
TO COMMON
CORE
ASSESSMENTS

**English
Language
Arts**

Mc
Graw
Hill
Education

Bothell, WA • Chicago, IL • Columbus, OH • New York, NY

www.mheonline.com

Send all inquiries to:
McGraw-Hill Education
Two Penn Plaza
New York, New York 10121

ISBN: 978-0-02-135105-3
MHID: 0-02-135105-8

Printed in the United States of America.

1 2 3 4 5 6 7 8 9 RHR 18 17 16 15 14 13

A

Table of Contents

Countdown to Common Core Assessments: English Language Arts

Countdown to Common Core Assessments: English Language Arts is an integral part of a complete assessment program aligned to the Common Core State Standards (CCSS). The advances in assessment featured in the Performance-Based Tasks and End-of-Year Assessment include passages and stimulus texts that reflect the increased text complexity and rigor required by the CCSS. The test items require higher-order thinking skills, emphasize the need for students to support responses with text evidence, and feature writing as the result of research, with prompts requiring student understanding of and engagement with the stimulus texts. In a departure from previous high-stakes assessments, individual items align to multiple standards.

NOTE: These tests are intended to familiarize students with the types of items they may encounter on the Common Core assessments. The test scores will provide you with a general idea of how well students have mastered the various skills; the scores are *not* intended to be used for classroom grading purposes.

Overview of Performance-Based Tasks

The Performance-Based Tasks provide students with scenarios that establish a unified purpose for reading and writing. Two distinct types of performance-based tasks are provided. The first five tasks are similar to the tasks students are likely to encounter in states that participate in the Partnership for Assessment of Readiness for College and Careers (PARCC) consortium. The second five tasks are similar to the tasks students are likely to encounter in states that participate in the Smarter Balanced Assessment Consortium.

All of the performance-based tasks provided in this book are appropriate for use in any state, whether consortia-affiliated or independent. Use these tasks in any combination to increase students' comfort level with and understanding of the range of CCSS assessments they may encounter.

Task and Item Types

All of the performance-based tasks assess student integration of knowledge and skills. Each task assesses multiple standards that address comprehension, research skills, genre writing, and the use of English language conventions. The stimulus texts and questions in each task build toward the goal of the final writing topic. Students write across texts to demonstrate their understanding of key elements underpinning the multiple sources.

Each PARCC-style assessment comprises three distinct tasks—**Narrative Writing, Literary Analysis,** and **Research Simulation.** Selected response items generally have two distinct parts. In Part A, students answer a text-based question; in Part B, they support their answer with evidence from the text. The Narrative Writing task uses a single stimulus passage; the Prose Constructed Response (PCR) asks students to complete or further develop the passage in a manner consistent with the existing story elements. PCR items in the Literary Analysis and Research Simulation tasks ask students to craft written essays in response to a variety of stimulus texts.

Each Smarter Balanced-style assessment consists of one of three distinct tasks—**Narrative, Opinion,** or **Informational.** The tasks employ a range of item types to measure student understanding. Research Questions include both selected-response and constructed-response items that test students' comprehension of the stimulus texts and help them to synthesize the information provided by the texts. Students then are directed to craft a written response to the texts and questions.

Administering and Scoring the Performance-Based Tasks

Administer each performance-based task separately. For planning purposes, use the suggested times given below.

- Allow 50 minutes for the Narrative Writing task, 80 minutes for the Literary Analysis task, and 80 minutes for the Research Simulation task.
- Allow 105 minutes for completion of each Narrative, Opinion, and Informational task. During the first 35 minutes, students will read the stimulus materials and answer the research questions; after a short break, students will use the remaining 70 minutes for planning, writing, and editing their responses.

Scoring the Selected-Response and Research Questions

Each Narrative Writing, Literary Analysis, and Research Simulation, selected-response item is worth 2 points.

Score two-part items as follows:

- 2 points if both Part A and Part B are correct
- 1 point if Part A is correct and Part B is incorrect or partially correct
- 0 points if Part A is incorrect, even if Part B is correct

Score one-part items as follows:

- 2 points if correct
- 1 point if partially correct
- 0 points if incorrect

For the Narrative, Opinion, and Informational task Research Questions, selected-response items are worth 1 point and constructed-response items are worth 2 points.

Scoring the Essays

Score the Narrative Writing, Literary Analysis, and Research Simulation PCRs holistically on a 16-point scale. Point values are broken down as follows:

- 3 points for addressing the relevant reading comprehension standards [R]
- 9 points for addressing the relevant writing standards [W]
- 4 points for addressing the relevant language conventions standards [L]

A PCR scoring rubric follows the Answer Keys to help you score the essays.

Score the Narrative, Opinion, and Informational task essays holistically on a 10-point scale. Point values are broken down as follows:

- 4 points for purpose/organization [P/O]
- 4 points for evidence/elaboration [E/E] or development/elaboration [D/E]
- 2 points for English language conventions [C]

Genre-specific scoring rubrics follow the Answer Keys to help you score the essays.

Answer Keys

In addition to the responses to the test items, the Answer Keys identify CCSS correlations. The Narrative, Opinion, and Informational task Answer Keys also identify claims and targets met, Depth of Knowledge (DOK), and level of difficulty. You can copy the Answer Keys and use them to track each student's scores.

Overview of End-of-Year Assessment

The End-of-Year Assessment focuses on reading and vocabulary skills, which are assessed by selected-response items. RI or RL standard 1 is the structural component underlying every comprehension item. Additional grade-level comprehension and vocabulary standards address the identification and use of supporting text evidence.

Administering and Scoring the End-of-Year Assessment

Administer the End-of-Year Assessment in two or three sessions, with a short break between each session. For planning purposes, allow 140 minutes per test, excluding the break periods.

Each of the 26 items is worth 2 points. The Answer Key provides a scoring column to create a 52-point test, with multi-part questions eligible for partial credit. In addition to the responses to the test items, the Answer Key identifies CCSS correlations. You can copy the Answer Key and use it to track each student's scores.

Score two-part items as follows:

- 2 points if both Part A and Part B are correct
- 1 point if Part A is correct and Part B is incorrect or partially correct
- 0 points if Part A is incorrect, even if Part B is correct

Score one-part items as follows:

- 2 points if correct
- 1 point if partially correct
- 0 points if incorrect

NOTE: If you prefer to give all items equal weight, give full credit only for completely correct answers and no credit for partially correct answers.

Narrative Writing 1

Today you will read the story "What Do We Do Now?" As you read, pay close attention to the plot and how the characters interact. You will answer questions to prepare to write a narrative story.

Read the story "What Do We Do Now?" and answer the questions that follow.

What Do We Do Now?

1   Carla hated to admit it, but Daddy was right. Actually, the thing that Carla really minded was the weather forecast. Carla had just kicked a goal when she felt the buzz of her cell phone. It was a text from Daddy. The storm was going to be worse than expected, and Carla had to come home immediately.

2   Carla was not surprised that she was the first one to be notified about the storm. Carla's father was a computer programmer who worked at home. As Daddy sat at the computer, news alerts popped up. Carla wondered how Daddy could stand looking at a screen all day. One time he had tried to explain. "It's fascinating. These symbols on my screen are a puzzle. When I write a program, I feel like a detective!" He enjoyed working from home, too. Carla liked that her father could adjust to anything.

3   When Carla arrived home, Daddy was waiting by the door. Carla found her younger brother and sister in the family room, in front of a huge screen. "Is it possible?" Carla asked playfully. "Haven't you two moved once since I went to play soccer?"

4   Joseph, who was 10, just laughed. Sunita, a 7-year old, looked at Carla and said, "We moved! That's silly. Carla, you love to play Desert Girl. Take my turn!"

5   "Desert Girl will have to wait," said another voice. It was Mama, who was back from the hospital, where she was a nurse. Mama must have left her job early to get home before the storm hit.

6   Carla was hopeful. Maybe Mama was giving them a "screen time out." Maybe they could finally play Wordle, which was her favorite game. Joseph and Sunita never wanted to play Wordle because it was a board game. This disappointed Carla. However, she had learned to enjoy the computer games that her brother and sister played.

GO ON →

7   "It's no time for games," Mama said. "The radio said the storm might cause blackouts. We need to get ready." Out of nowhere, Mama began producing pieces of paper and handing them out. Carla should have expected this, since Mama had a list for every occasion.

8   All three kids had the same list. Their job was to unplug appliances, such as computers and televisions, which could be harmed by power surges. "Why?" Sunita wailed. "Can't we leave one to play on?"

9   "No," Joseph said, surprising Carla. "We don't need the computer, because *this* can be a game. We can get points for each appliance on the list." The list had sixteen items, and as Carla crossed out the last item, a flash of lightning went through the sky. Seconds later, there was a crack of thunder. The lights flickered and then went out. Carla turned on the flashlight her mother had given her.

10   "What do we do now?" Sunita asked.

11   Carla turned the flashlight toward the toy chest. "Looks like we will need another game to play," she said, grinning.

GO ON →

1 **Part A:** What is the meaning of the word **forecast** as it is used in paragraph 1?

   Ⓐ prediction

   Ⓑ climate

   Ⓒ response

   Ⓓ memory

Part B: Which phrase from paragraph 1 helps the reader understand the meaning of **forecast**?

   Ⓐ "... hated to admit it, but Daddy was right."

   Ⓑ "... the thing that Carla really minded ..."

   Ⓒ "... when she felt the buzz of her cell phone."

   Ⓓ "... storm was going to be worse than expected ..."

2 **Part A:** What happened after Carla felt the buzz of her cell phone?

   Ⓐ She scored a goal.

   Ⓑ She had to go home.

   Ⓒ She heard the weather forecast.

   Ⓓ Her friends left the soccer field.

Part B: Which detail from the story shows the cause of the event in Part A?

   Ⓐ A storm was coming.

   Ⓑ The electricity went out.

   Ⓒ Carla's brother and sister were playing a game.

   Ⓓ Carla's mother came home from work with a list.

GO ON →

3 **Part A:** Which of the following sentences **best** states the story's theme?

(A) To get along well with others, people have to change.

(B) Planning for the future is important for survival.

(C) People must be able to respond to and deal with new situations.

(D) Life is a puzzle, and figuring it out can be fun.

Part B: Which detail from the story is important to the story's theme?

(A) "Carla wondered how Daddy could stand looking at a screen all day." (Paragraph 2)

(B) "Carla liked that her father could adjust to anything." (Paragraph 2)

(C) "Maybe Mama was giving them a 'screen time out.'" (Paragraph 6)

(D) "Maybe they could finally play Wordle, which was her favorite game." (Paragraph 6)

GO ON →

4 **Part A:** Which phrase below **best** describes Daddy's character?

(A) prepared and strict

(B) excitable and angry

(C) caring and dependable

(D) disorganized and kind

Part B: Which sentence from the story supports the phrase you selected in Part A?

(A) "As Daddy sat at the computer, news alerts popped up." (Paragraph 2)

(B) "These symbols on my screen are a puzzle." (Paragraph 2)

(C) "When I write a program, I feel like a detective!" (Paragraph 2)

(D) "When Carla arrived home, Daddy was waiting by the door." (Paragraph 3)

5 **Part A:** Read paragraph 7 below. Underline **two** details that show Mama's response to the storm.

> "It's no time for games," Mama said. "The radio said the storm might cause blackouts. We need to get ready." Out of nowhere, Mama began producing pieces of paper and handing them out. Carla should have expected this, since Mama had a list for every occasion.

Part B: What is the effect of Mama's response to the storm?

(A) Daddy sends Carla a text message about the storm.

(B) The children turn out the lights.

(C) The children unplug all the appliances.

(D) Carla gives the other children a "screen time out."

GO ON →

6 In the story, the author established a family of characters who are faced with a problem. Think about the details the author used to create the plot and the characters. The narrative ends before the family has resolved the problem caused by the storm.

Write an ending for the story that shows how the characters resolve their problem. Be sure to use what you know about Carla, the other characters, the plot, and the theme to tell what happens next. Use the space below to plan your writing. Write your story on a separate sheet of paper.

Grade 4 • Performance-Based Tasks

Narrative Writing 2

Today you will read the article "A World of Sand." As you read the text, you will gather information and answer questions about a sand-sculpting competition so that you can write a narrative description.

Read the article "A World of Sand" and answer the questions that follow.

A World of Sand

1   Every November, 65,000 artists and fans travel to Fort Myers Beach, Florida, for a summery event: the American Sand Sculpting Championship. The festival has been happening for more than 25 years. This makes it one of the world's longest-running sand-sculpting competitions.

2   Anyone can enter the competition. One division is for professional sand sculptors. That's right—there are actually people who travel around the world and build sculptures of sand as their job! In 2013, the professionals at the festival will come from nine U.S. states and ten countries. There are also amateur divisions for kids, families, and other people with little or no sculpting experience.

3   According to the artists, Fort Myers Beach has perfect sand for sculpting because it is very fine. The extremely small grains pack together and hold wetness well. By the end of the festival, competitors mold more than a thousand tons of sand into 30 works of art.

4   We're not just talking about sand castles here. One past award winner is a sculpture of the human brain called "Minded." Winter themes are also popular at the festival. One year, two of the top sculptures were titled "Old Man Winter" and "Snow Queen."

5   There are many activities in addition to watching the main competition. For instance, spectators can take lessons in sand sculpting. They can also check out speed sculpting. In this event, professional artists race to complete the best sculpture in a ten-minute "sculpt-off." With a whole beach of sand, the choices are endless!

GO ON →

1 **Part A:** What does the word **amateur** mean as it is used in paragraph 2?

(A) judge

(B) spectator

(C) beginner

(D) painter

Part B: Which phrase from the article helps the reader understand the meaning of **amateur**?

(A) ". . . people who . . . build sculptures of sand as their job!" (Paragraph 2)

(B) ". . . other people with little or no . . . experience." (Paragraph 2)

(C) ". . . extremely small grains pack together . . ." (Paragraph 3)

(D) ". . . spectators can take lessons. . . ." (Paragraph 5)

GO ON →

2 **Part A:** Which word **best** describes the sand-sculpting competition that takes place at Fort Myers Beach every year?

(A) amateur

(B) international

(C) small

(D) formal

Part B: Which phrase from the article supports the answer to Part A?

(A) "... 65,000 artists and fans travel ..." (Paragraph 1)

(B) "... nine U.S. states and ten countries." (Paragraph 2)

(C) "By the end of the festival ..." (Paragraph 3)

(D) "... titled 'Old Man Winter' ..." (Paragraph 4)

GO ON →

3 **Part A:** What type of evidence does the author provide to support the point that the sand at Fort Myers Beach is "perfect" for sculpting?

(A) interviews with judges of the competition

(B) statistics about the size of the sand grains

(C) opinions from professional sand sculptors

(D) experiences of visitors to the competition

Part B: Which phrase from paragraph 3 **best** supports the answer to Part A?

(A) "According to the artists . . ."

(B) ". . . because it is very fine."

(C) ". . . hold wetness well."

(D) ". . . more than a thousand tons . . ."

GO ON →

4 **Part A:** What is the overall structure of most paragraphs in the article?

Ⓐ general statement followed by examples

Ⓑ problem and several possible solutions

Ⓒ chronological list of events

Ⓓ causes and their effects

Part B: Which sentence from the article supports the answer to Part A?

Ⓐ "This makes it one of the world's longest-running sand-sculpting competitions." (Paragraph 1)

Ⓑ "According to the artists, Fort Myers Beach has perfect sand for sculpting because it is very fine." (Paragraph 3)

Ⓒ "One past award winner is a sculpture of the human brain called 'Minded.'" (Paragraph 4)

Ⓓ "For instance, spectators can take lessons in sand sculpting." (Paragraph 5)

GO ON →

5 Underline the **two** sentences from paragraph 2 that **best** support the idea that a wide range of people can enjoy the American Sand Sculpting Championship.

> Anyone can enter the competition. One division is for professional sand sculptors. That's right—there are actually people who travel around the world and build sculptures of sand as their job! In 2013, the professionals at the festival will come from nine U.S. states and ten countries. There are also amateur divisions for kids, families, and other people with little or no sculpting experience.

GO ON →

Name: _____ Date: _____

6 A class is researching the topic "Family-friendly events in the United States." The goal is to study regular events that are enjoyable for people of all ages to experience. You are assigned to narrate and describe the American Sand Sculpting Championship.

Use the article "A World of Sand" to write a narrative. Share what it is like to experience this competition as a family. To create a well-written narrative:

- Use details from the article to support your description of the American Sand Sculpting Championship. Any inferences you draw should be supported by text evidence.

- Organize the narrative to make important connections between the activities at the festival and the descriptive details you include.

- Use narrative techniques where appropriate, such as point of view and suspense, to make sure readers understand the excitement of the activities at the competition.

Use the space below to plan your writing. Write your narrative on a separate sheet of paper.

STOP

Literary Analysis 1

Today you will read a passage taken from *The Wonderful Wizard of Oz*. You will also read a poem titled "An Indian Summer Day on the Prairie." As you read, think about where the passage and the poem take place. You will be asked to write about how the authors used the same setting in different ways.

Read the passage from *The Wonderful Wizard of Oz* and answer the questions that follow.

Most of the novel The Wonderful Wizard of Oz *is set in a place that is very different from anything the main character, Dorothy, has ever experienced. In this passage, Dorothy is at home with her aunt and uncle on their farm in Kansas, just before her journey begins.*

from *The Wonderful Wizard of Oz*

by L. Frank Baum

1   When Dorothy stood in the doorway and looked around, she could see nothing but the great gray prairie on every side. Not a tree nor a house broke the broad sweep of flat country that reached to the edge of the sky in all directions. The sun had baked the plowed land into a gray mass, with little cracks running through it. Even the grass was not green, for the sun had burned the tops of the long blades until they were the same gray color to be seen everywhere. Once the house had been painted, but the sun blistered the paint and the rains washed it away, and now the house was as dull and gray as everything else.

2   When Aunt Em came there to live she was a young, pretty wife. The sun and wind had changed her, too. They had taken the sparkle from her eyes and left them a sober gray; they had taken the red from her cheeks and lips, and they were gray also. She was thin and gaunt, and never smiled now. When Dorothy, who was an orphan, first came to her, Aunt Em had been so startled by the child's laughter that she would scream and press her hand upon her heart whenever Dorothy's merry voice reached her ears; and she still looked at the little girl with wonder that she could find anything to laugh at.

GO ON →

3   Uncle Henry never laughed. He worked hard from morning till night and did not know what joy was. He was gray also, from his long beard to his rough boots, and he looked stern and solemn, and rarely spoke.

4   It was Toto that made Dorothy laugh, and saved her from growing as gray as her other surroundings. Toto was not gray; he was a little black dog, with long silky hair and small black eyes that twinkled merrily on either side of his funny, wee nose. Toto played all day long, and Dorothy played with him, and loved him dearly.

5   Today, however, they were not playing. Uncle Henry sat upon the doorstep and looked anxiously at the sky, which was even grayer than usual. Dorothy stood in the door with Toto in her arms, and looked at the sky too. Aunt Em was washing the dishes.

6   From the far north they heard a low wail of the wind, and Uncle Henry and Dorothy could see where the long grass bowed in waves before the coming storm. There now came a sharp whistling in the air from the south, and as they turned their eyes that way they saw ripples in the grass coming from that direction also.

7   Suddenly Uncle Henry stood up.

8   "There's a cyclone coming, Em," he called to his wife. "I'll go look after the stock." Then he ran toward the sheds where the cows and horses were kept.

9   Aunt Em dropped her work and came to the door. One glance told her of the danger close at hand.

10   "Quick, Dorothy!" she screamed. "Run for the cellar!"

11   Toto jumped out of Dorothy's arms and hid under the bed, and the girl started to get him. Aunt Em, badly frightened, threw open the trap door in the floor and climbed down the ladder into the small, dark hole. Dorothy caught Toto at last and started to follow her aunt. When she was halfway across the room there came a great shriek from the wind, and the house shook so hard that she lost her footing and sat down suddenly upon the floor.

12   Then a strange thing happened.

GO ON →

Grade 4 • Performance-Based Tasks

Copyright © McGraw-Hill Education

13   The house whirled around two or three times and rose slowly through the air. Dorothy felt as if she were going up in a balloon.

14   The north and south winds met where the house stood, and made it the exact center of the cyclone. In the middle of a cyclone the air is generally still, but the great pressure of the wind on every side of the house raised it up higher and higher, until it was at the very top of the cyclone; and there it remained and was carried miles and miles away as easily as you could carry a feather.

15   It was very dark, and the wind howled horribly around her, but Dorothy found she was riding quite easily. After the first few whirls around, and one other time when the house tipped badly, she felt as if she were being rocked gently, like a baby in a cradle.

16   Toto did not like it. He ran about the room, now here, now there, barking loudly; but Dorothy sat quite still on the floor and waited to see what would happen.

GO ON →

Grade 4 • Performance-Based Tasks

1 **Part A:** What does the word **prairie** mean as it is used in paragraph 1?

(A) type of weather

(B) wooden house

(C) land with few trees

(D) border of the sky

Part B: Read this excerpt from paragraph 1. Underline the phrase that helps the reader understand the meaning of **prairie**.

> When Dorothy stood in the doorway and looked around, she could see nothing but the great gray prairie on every side. Not a tree nor a house broke the broad sweep of flat country that reached to the edge of the sky in all directions. The sun had baked the plowed land into a gray mass, with little cracks running through it. Even the grass was not green, for the sun had burned the tops of the long blades until they were the same gray color to be seen everywhere. . . .

GO ON →

2 **Part A:** How does the author connect the setting and the characters in the passage?

(A) by describing what the characters look like

(B) by telling what Aunt Em and Uncle Henry do to stay safe during the cyclone

(C) by explaining exactly how the cyclone lifts the house

(D) by repeating the word *gray* to describe both the setting and the characters

Part B: Which **two** of the following provide evidence that supports your answer in Part A?

(A) "Once the house had been painted, but the sun blistered the paint and the rains washed it away. . . ." (Paragraph 1)

(B) "The sun and wind had changed her, too. . . . She was thin and gaunt, and never smiled now." (Paragraph 2)

(C) "He was gray also, from his long beard to his rough boots, and he looked stern and solemn, and rarely spoke." (Paragraph 3)

(D) "Uncle Henry sat upon the doorstep and looked anxiously at the sky, which was even grayer than usual." (Paragraph 5)

(E) "Dorothy stood in the door with Toto in her arms, and looked at the sky too. Aunt Em was washing the dishes." (Paragraph 5)

(F) "The north and south winds met where the house stood, and made it the exact center of the cyclone." (Paragraph 14)

GO ON →

3 **Part A:** Which of the following states a theme of the passage?

Ⓐ Dorothy shares a happy home with Aunt Em and
Uncle Henry.

Ⓑ Flying through the air in a house is an everyday event.

Ⓒ Life on the prairie can be lonely and difficult.

Ⓓ It is important to sit still when something unusual happens.

Part B: Which sentence from the passage supports your answer?

Ⓐ "He worked hard from morning till night and did not know what
joy was." (Paragraph 3)

Ⓑ "Toto played all day long, and Dorothy played with him, and
loved him dearly." (Paragraph 4)

Ⓒ "From the far north they heard a low wail of the wind, and Uncle
Henry and Dorothy could see where the long grass bowed in
waves before the coming storm." (Paragraph 6)

Ⓓ "Aunt Em, badly frightened, threw open the trap door in the
floor and climbed down the ladder into the small, dark hole."
(Paragraph 11)

GO ON →

Read the poem "An Indian Summer Day on the Prairie" and answer the questions that follow.

An Indian Summer Day on the Prairie

by Vachel Lindsay

    (IN THE BEGINNING)

    The sun is a huntress young,

    The sun is a red, red joy,

    The sun is an Indian girl,

5   Of the tribe of the Illinois.

    (MID-MORNING)

    The sun is a smouldering fire,

    That creeps through the high gray plain,

    And leaves not a bush of cloud

10   To blossom with flowers of rain.

    (NOON)

    The sun is a wounded deer,

    That treads pale grass in the skies,

    Shaking his golden horns,

15   Flashing his baleful eyes.

    (SUNSET)

    The sun is an eagle old,

    There in the windless west.

    Atop of the spirit-cliffs

20   He builds him a crimson nest.

GO ON →

4 **Part A:** What does the phrase **crimson nest** mean in line 20?

Ⓐ Eagles like to build nests.

Ⓑ It describes the look of sunset.

Ⓒ The sun is different things to different people.

Ⓓ The sun is red all through the day.

Part B: Draw a line to match the description of the sun with the time of day.

sunrise	smouldering fire
morning	golden horns
noon	red, red joy

5 **Part A:** How does the poet create the idea that the sun is the main character in the poem?

Ⓐ by repeating the sun's name in most lines

Ⓑ by describing the sun as a creeping fire

Ⓒ by using different images to describe the sun

Ⓓ by dividing the poem into four stanzas

Part B: Which line from the poem is evidence that supports your answer?

Ⓐ "The sun is an Indian girl," (Line 4)

Ⓑ "Of the tribe of the Illinois." (Line 5)

Ⓒ "There in the windless west." (Line 18)

Ⓓ "Atop of the spirit-cliffs" (Line 19)

GO ON →

6 **Part A:** How do the headings of each stanza (lines 1, 6, 11, and 16) help the reader understand the structure of the poem?

(A) They describe the changing seasons.

(B) They tell how the sun and the prairie are the same.

(C) They separate the color words from their descriptions.

(D) They show that time is passing.

Part B: What **two** themes are found in the poem?

(A) Summer is the best time of year.

(B) The sun goes through many changes during a single day.

(C) There are many types of weather on the prairie.

(D) The sun is important to life on the prairie.

(E) Animals and people can live together on the prairie.

(F) Both a day and a person's life move through stages.

7 Both the passage from *The Wizard of Oz* and "An Indian Summer Day on the Prairie" are set on the prairie. Write an essay that compares how the texts use the prairie setting in different ways. In your essay, be sure to use important details from both texts, such as color words, to describe what the prairie looks like. Organize your essay to compare the setting in each text. Use the space below to plan your writing. Write your essay on a separate sheet of paper.

Literary Analysis 2

Today you will read and think about the story "Life After the Epidemic" and the poem "The Bluebird's Song." As you read these texts, you will gather information and answer questions about the themes of the texts so that you can write about the two themes.

Read the story "Life After the Epidemic" and answer the questions that follow.

Life After the Epidemic

1   "Epidemic!" Sandra wailed, her hands cradling her forehead. "I can't believe I lost on *epidemic*. I *know* that one!"

2   Sandra had won Clark Grammar School's spelling bee two years in a row, but today, although she was at the top of the school in the sixth grade, she had lost to Karen Lodge.

3   Sandra had been the model runner-up. She hadn't cried or looked sour during the awards ceremony, and she had even managed to give Karen a congratulatory smile.

4   Now, in the car with her mom, dad, and little brother John, she was letting out her disappointment. "I'm a fallen champion," Sandra declared. "I will forever remember 1962 as the year that I lost the spelling bee."

5   Mom and Dad gave each other a knowing smile and stayed quiet. John put his hand on his sister's shoulder and said, "It'll be okay, Sandy-bee."

6   "No more calling me Sandy-bee," Sandra snapped. "I don't deserve it. *Nobody* spells *epidemic* E-P-A! What was I thinking? It's so easy—like epigraph, epitaph, epicenter . . . the third letter is *I*. I bet they've even taught you that in fourth grade already, Johnny."

7   "No," John responded encouragingly, "I don't know any of those words."

8   "Well, I still bet you would have spelled them correctly."

9   Sandra turned her attention to the trees whizzing past under the cloudy sky, which reminded her of the gloom filling her mind.

10   Finally, Sandra broke the silence. "You know what?" she said. "I think it was an epidemic of forgetfulness that made me lose the spelling bee. It was something I caught, just like a cold—and now I'm worried I'll never recover."

GO ON →

11   "Sandra, I know you're upset, but you're being a bit dramatic," said Mom.

12   "I like to win, too," said John cheerfully, "but, Sandy, just think about it. Everybody thought you would win this year, and everyone talked about it. You were really nervous before this one. Next year, Karen will be the nervous one. You'll work hard, but you'll be calm."

13   "That's right," Dad agreed. "There will be less pressure, which gives you the advantage."

14   Sandra shrugged. "I guess so."

15   John continued. "Also, people get bored when the same person wins every year, and so it will be even more exciting if you come from behind and take the trophy again next year. People will say, 'Sandra did it again!' Don't you see? There's always another bee!"

16   Sandra thought about John's ideas. She was still afraid that the "illness" she'd caught would never heal. Next year, when she was in junior high, the words would be even harder. There would be more rules to study, more prefixes and roots and suffixes to know. And the competition would be tougher—students from three different schools attended Miller Junior High. On the other hand, John had made some reasonable points. Next year she wouldn't have to worry about being the reigning champion. And a victory would mean a lot more in a school of 650 than it had in a school of 225. She would drill herself on the words until she'd memorized every last one.

17   "John, you're right," said Sandra, ruffling her brother's hair. "You've convinced me that there *will* be life after the epidemic!"

GO ON →

     Grade 4 • **Performance-Based Tasks**

1 Select **three** details from the story that give a clue about the meaning of the word **epidemic**. Write the details in the graphic organizer.

Details

". . . her hands cradling her forehead." (Paragraph 1)

"I bet they've even taught you that . . ." (Paragraph 6)

". . . something I caught, just like a cold . . ." (Paragraph 10)

". . . worried I'll never recover." (Paragraph 10)

". . . you're being a bit dramatic . . ." (Paragraph 11)

". . . afraid that the 'illness' she'd caught would never heal." (Paragraph 16)

". . . victory would mean a lot more in a school of 650 . . ." (Paragraph 16)

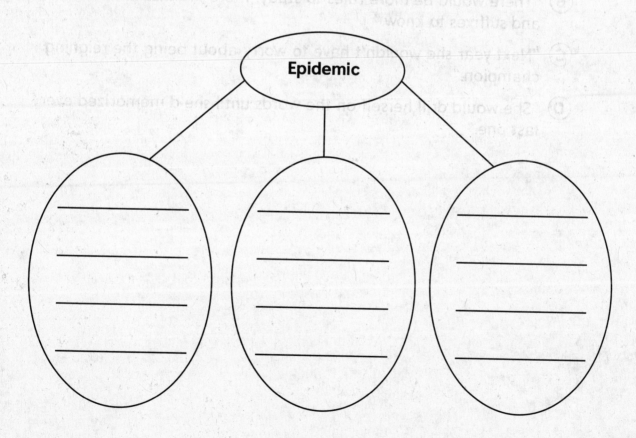

Epidemic

GO ON →

2 **Part A:** Which statement **best** describes Sandra?

(A) She wants to be perfect, and so she is hard on herself when she makes mistakes.

(B) She becomes very angry when she loses and does not want to listen to others.

(C) She is likely to get in a disagreement with her brother when he offers her advice.

(D) She refuses to change her mind once she has decided how she feels about something.

Part B: Which sentence in paragraph 16 supports your response in Part A?

(A) "Next year, when she was in junior high, the words would be even harder."

(B) "There would be more rules to study, more prefixes and roots and suffixes to know."

(C) "Next year she wouldn't have to worry about being the reigning champion."

(D) "She would drill herself on the words until she'd memorized every last one."

3 **Part A:** What lesson does Sandra learn in the story?

(A) Schoolwork should be the top priority.

(B) Something positive can come from disappointment.

(C) People do not always say what you expect them to.

(D) Older siblings can be good role models.

Part B: Which sentence from the story **best** shows this same lesson?

(A) "I *know* that one!" (Paragraph 1)

(B) "Sandra had been the model runner-up." (Paragraph 3)

(C) "There's always another bee!" (Paragraph 15)

(D) "'John, you're right,' said Sandra, ruffling her brother's hair." (Paragraph 17)

GO ON →

Read the poem "The Bluebird's Song" and answer the questions that follow.

The Bluebird's Song

by Emily Huntington Miller

I know the song that the bluebird is singing,

Out in the apple tree where he is swinging.

Brave little fellow! the skies may be dreary—

Nothing cares he while his heart is so cheery.

5 Hark! how the music leaps out from his throat!

Hark! was there ever so merry a note?

Listen a while, and you'll hear what he's saying,

Up in the apple tree swinging and swaying.

"Dear little blossoms down under the snow,

10 You must be weary of winter I know.

Listen, I'll sing you a message of cheer!

Summer is coming! and springtime is here!

"Little white snowdrop! I pray you arise;

Bright yellow crocus! please open your eyes;

15 Sweet little violets, hid from the cold,

Put on your **mantles**[1] of purple and gold;

Daffodils! Daffodils! say, do you hear?—

Summer is coming, and springtime is here!"

---

mantles[1]—things that cover; cloaks

GO ON →

④ Part A: What is the meaning of the word **dreary** as it is used in line 3 of the poem?

(A) filled with lightning

(B) difficult to see

(C) colorless and lifeless

(D) mysterious and exciting

Part B: Which **two** lines or phrases from the poem help the reader understand the meaning of **dreary**?

(A) "Out in the apple tree where he is swinging." (Line 2)

(B) "Nothing cares he while his heart is so cheery." (Line 4)

(C) "Listen a while, and you'll hear . . ." (Line 7)

(D) ". . . down under the snow" (Line 9)

(E) ". . . yellow crocus! please open your eyes" (Line 14)

(F) ". . . Daffodils! say, do you hear?" (Line 17)

GO ON →

5 How do lines 15–16 show that "The Bluebird's Song" is a poem instead of a prose story? Write each detail in the correct box to compare and contrast poetry and prose.

Details

The words at the ends of the lines rhyme.

The lines are spoken by a character.

Each line talks about a color.

Both lines are about a type of flower.

Each line has the same rhythm.

The two lines are part of a stanza.

Elements of Poetry	Elements of Both Poetry and Prose
_____	_____
_____	_____
_____	_____
_____	_____
_____	_____

GO ON →

6 **Part A:** What is a theme of the poem?

(A) Singing a song is the best way to make spring come early.

(B) People will never be able to understand nature.

(C) The growth of flowers is like the coming of winter.

(D) Even in dark times, there are reasons to be happy.

Part B: Which lines from the poem **best** show this theme?

(A) lines 3–4

(B) lines 5–6

(C) lines 9–10

(D) lines 15–16

GO ON →

7 "Life After the Epidemic" and "The Bluebird's Song" have similar themes, or lessons. Write an essay that compares and contrasts the themes of the story and the poem. In your essay, be sure to:

- Use important details from both the story and the poem to explain how the themes are similar and different. Any inferences you draw should be supported by text evidence.

- Organize your ideas to compare and contrast the themes of each text.

Use the space below to plan your writing. Write your essay on a separate sheet of paper.

Research Simulation

There are interesting materials all around us. Today you will research some of these materials and how they are used. You will read an article about some materials with special characteristics. Then you will read an article about concrete.

As you read these texts, you will gather information and answer questions about the materials. Then you will be asked to write an essay about them.

Read the article "Tomorrow's Materials" and answer the questions that follow.

Tomorrow's Materials

1   It is common to see buildings made of wood, spoons made of metal, and clothing made of cotton. All of these materials have been used for many years because they are strong and available in nature. But scientists and inventors are always looking for new materials to make useful objects. Let's take a look at two of tomorrow's materials. They just might amaze you.

2   Our first material of tomorrow is called Neptune balls, also known as sea balls. They are made of Neptune grass, a type of seaweed found in the Mediterranean Sea. Pieces of dead Neptune grass get rolled into balls in the waves, and then the balls wash up on the shore. They are a common sight on the beach, but nobody thought they were useful until recently. Somebody studied Neptune balls closely and decided to try using them as insulation.

3   Insulation is a material that keeps something from losing heat. People put insulation inside the walls of houses to help keep them warm inside. Neptune balls work very well as insulation. They keep heat from escaping. In addition, they do not rot or grow mold, and they do not catch on fire. Neptune balls are totally natural and found easily on beaches. Nobody uses them for anything else. Today, Neptune balls are collected in the countries of Albania and Tunisia. Then a company in Germany shakes the sand from the balls, chops them into smaller pieces, and sells the material.

4   Next, we will explore a material that can be found not just in one sea but all over the world. It's spider silk! For centuries some people have used spider silk as a material. For instance, it has served as fishing line and in bandages for cuts.

GO ON →

Scientists are now trying to make a material that acts in exactly the same way. They believe that this material would be very profitable. However, nobody has been able to gather large amounts of spider silk for human use. Small amounts will never make much money.

5   Why do people want to use spider silk? First, it is extremely strong. A piece of spider silk is about five times stronger than a piece of steel of the same weight. Some experts say that a spider web with strands as thick as a pencil could stop a jumbo jet in flight! Second, spider silk is very flexible. You can stretch a strand by nearly half of its original length. Finally, spider silk is lightweight. Inventors are always searching for materials with these qualities.

6   Spider silk could be used to make strong but flexible car parts, such as bumpers and airbags. Sponges and long-lasting clothing are other possibilities for this material. These are only a few of the ideas that have come up.

7   Tomorrow, or perhaps next year, you just might hear more about Neptune balls or spider silk. In fact, you might have seaweed to thank for keeping you warm inside on a cold day. And you might have a spider to thank for a coat that lasts for many years. Stay on the lookout!

GO ON →

1 **Part A:** What is the meaning of the word **profitable** as it is used in paragraph 4?

Ⓐ able to be collected

Ⓑ good for making money

Ⓒ copied by humans

Ⓓ available in nature

Part B: Which phrase from the article describes the opposite of the word **profitable**?

Ⓐ "... and sells the material." (Paragraph 3)

Ⓑ "... not just in one sea ..." (Paragraph 4)

Ⓒ "... never make much money." (Paragraph 4)

Ⓓ "... materials with these qualities." (Paragraph 5)

GO ON →

2 Organize the statements in the box to show the overall structure of paragraph 3. First, write the main idea in the correct part of the chart. Then, write the four supporting details in the order they appear.

Statements:

Neptune balls do not rot or grow mold.

Neptune balls are a helpful, useful material.

Neptune balls do not catch on fire.

Neptune balls keep heat from escaping.

Neptune balls are easily found in nature.

Main Idea	Supporting Details
	1.
	2.
	3.
	4.

GO ON →

3 **Part A:** According to the author, what is the main reason why people want to gather large amounts of spider silk?

(A) It is very strong.

(B) It is made by an animal.

(C) It has been used before.

(D) It traps heat inside.

Part B: What evidence does the author include to support the answer to Part A?

(A) Spider silk can be used to make sponges.

(B) Spider silk has strands as thick as a pencil.

(C) Spider silk is extremely flexible.

(D) Spider silk is much stronger than steel.

GO ON →

4 The author does not always clearly state the main idea of a text. Drawing on the information in "Tomorrow's Materials," write an essay that summarizes the article's main idea and gives examples of how the author supports that idea.

Remember to use text evidence to support your ideas. Use the space below to plan your writing. Write your essay on a separate sheet of paper.

GO ON →

Read the article "Feats of Concrete" and answer the questions that follow.

Feats of Concrete

1   Imagine a world without concrete. People everywhere would have no sidewalks to walk on. Thousands of roads and highways would vanish. Entire buildings would disappear or crumble. Rivers would burst with water that was once held back by dams.

2   If you ever doubt the importance of concrete as a building material, consider this fact: people use concrete two times more than steel, plastic, aluminum, and wood combined!

3   The ancient Romans were most likely the first people to use concrete. They figured out a way to improve cement, an ingredient in concrete. Natural cement is made of lime, which comes from limestone, plus ash from volcanoes. However, many companies today make synthetic cement.

4   Making and using concrete is fairly simple. Here is the process:

A. Mix crushed stone, sand, or gravel with cement and water. In general, the less water you use, the stronger the concrete will be.

B. Pour concrete into the shape you want it to take.

C. Let the concrete dry slowly and fully by keeping it damp.

5   Why is concrete such a widely used material? First, it is amazingly strong. For example, the Pantheon, a building in Rome, has been around for almost 1,900 years. Hundreds of people visit this building every day. The Hoover Dam, on the border of Nevada and Arizona, is also made of concrete. It is strong enough to hold back the Colorado River. Second, concrete can be used to make a wide variety of objects. You can find it in buildings, bridges, sidewalks, roads, boats, works of art, flowerpots, fountains, and thousands more items. Our world would look very different without it.

GO ON →

Copyright © McGraw-Hill Education

5 **Part A:** What does the word **synthetic** mean as it is used in paragraph 3?

Ⓐ new and updated

Ⓑ mixed with ash

Ⓒ made of stone

Ⓓ not found in nature

Part B: Which context clue best helps the reader understand the meaning of **synthetic**?

Ⓐ "The ancient Romans were . . . the first people to use . . ." (Paragraph 3)

Ⓑ ". . . a way to improve cement . . ." (Paragraph 3)

Ⓒ "Natural cement . . . However, . . ." (Paragraph 3)

Ⓓ ". . . using concrete is fairly simple." (Paragraph 4)

GO ON →

6 **Part A:** Which step in making concrete comes first?

(A) Pour out the concrete.

(B) Mix sand, cement, and water.

(C) Let the concrete dry.

(D) Keep the concrete damp.

Part B: Once the concrete is made, what is the last step in using it?

(A) Add water to the gravel.

(B) Allow it to dry completely.

(C) Pour it into the shape you want.

(D) Mix it with natural cement.

GO ON →

7 Draw a line to match each paragraph number in the left column with the letter of the correct main idea in the right column.

Paragraph   Main Idea

1   A. Concrete is very strong and can be used for many different products.

2   B. You can make and use concrete through three simple steps.

3   C. People use far more concrete for building than other common materials.

4   D. Concrete is a major part of the world we see around us.

5   E. Concrete was probably invented when ancient Romans mixed cement and ash.

8 You have read two texts about different materials. Both provide information about where the materials come from and how they are useful to people. The two texts are:

• "Tomorrow's Materials"
• "Feats of Concrete"

Think about how each author describes the sources and uses of the materials.

Write an essay that compares and contrasts where the materials in the texts come from and how they are used. Remember to use text evidence to support your ideas. Use the space below to plan your writing. Write your essay on a separate sheet of paper.

Narrative 1

Student Directions

Task:

Your class is learning about folktales. Your teacher has asked you to write an original folktale. Before you write your story, you will read two folktales from different cultures. You will also read an informational article that tells about the characteristics of folktales.

After you have looked at these sources, you will answer some questions about them. Briefly scan the sources and the three questions that follow. Then, go back and read the sources carefully to gain the information you will need to answer the questions and write an original folktale.

In Part 2, you will write an original folktale using what you have learned from the two folktales and the informational article.

Directions for Part 1

You will now read two folktales and one article. You can look at any of the sources as often as you like.

Research Questions:

After looking at the folktales and the article, use the rest of the time in Part 1 to answer three questions about them. Your answers to these questions will be scored. Also, your answers will help you think about what you have learned about folktales, which should help you write your own folktale.

You may refer to the folktales and the article when you think it would be helpful. You may also look at your notes. Answer the questions in the space provided.

GO ON →

The Purse of One Hundred Coins

a Jewish folktale

There was once a merchant who lost a purse of 100 gold coins. The merchant announced, "I will give a reward to anyone who finds my lost purse!"

It just so happened that a beggar came upon the lost purse while walking along the market road. Looking inside, he saw that it had 100 gold pieces. When he stepped into the marketplace he heard the merchant crying, "A reward for my lost purse!"

The beggar was an honest man, and so he handed the purse to the merchant and kindly asked for his reward. The merchant scowled at the beggar and looked inside his purse.

"This purse had 200 gold pieces," the merchant lied. "How dare you ask for a reward when you've already taken 100 pieces from it!"

The beggar was insulted by the merchant's words and said that he was an honest man. He demanded to take the matter to the court. And so the judge listened first to the merchant and then to the beggar. At last, he said, "I believe you both. I believe that the merchant lost a purse that had 200 gold coins in it. And, I believe that the beggar found a purse that had 100 gold coins. Therefore, the beggar must not have found the merchant's purse."

The judge gave the purse to the truthful beggar, and the untruthful merchant left the court empty-handed.

GO ON →

The Wild Goose

a folktale from China

There were once two hunters in a field who saw a fat goose. The first hunter said, "That goose will taste delicious roasted with potatoes and apples." His mouth watered at the thought of it golden brown in the oven. Raising his bow and arrow, he aimed carefully at the bird flying above.

"Don't be ridiculous!" the other hunter shouted suddenly. "That would be a waste of such a fine bird. Why, everyone knows that it should be cut up and mixed in a stew. It would last longer that way and be able to feed more people."

The first hunter lowered his bow and arrow and argued with the other hunter for quite some time. Finally, they decided to go to their clan leader. "He will know what is best," said the first hunter.

And so the hunters took their disagreement to the leader, who settled the discussion by telling the men to roast half of the goose and to cook the other half in a stew. This pleased both hunters, for they each had gotten what they wanted. The only problem was that when they returned to the same hunting spot, the goose had long since flown away!

GO ON →

Characteristics of a Folktale

A folktale is a traditional story that has been passed down from generation to generation. It is a fictional story. However, sometimes it can also be considered part nonfiction. That is because folktales are based on the customs and beliefs of the cultures they come from. The people who originally made up the story truly believed in it. They may also have partly based the folktale on some real event.

Folktales usually explain something about the world or teach an important lesson about life. They often use everyday people to explain how to act or behave. Sometimes they have magical or supernatural elements, but these elements are not necessary.

Folktales take on the characteristics of the time and place in which they are told. For this reason, folktales may change through the years so that people in different time periods can understand them. Still, folktales always have universal themes that people around the world can understand.

Folktale Characteristics:

- Traditional stories that sometimes have modern updates
- Try to explain something about the world or teach an important lesson
- May have magical elements
- Relate to the beliefs and customs of a culture
- Have universal themes
- Help others understand the world around them

GO ON →

Research Questions

1 How are the "The Purse of One Hundred Coins" and "The Wild Goose" alike?

(A) Both follow the same pattern of events that include a conflict and resolution.

(B) Both teach the same lesson about being honest to others.

(C) Both present customs and beliefs from the same culture.

(D) Both include some magical elements.

2 How do you know that the two stories you just read are folktales? Support your answer with details from the article and the folktales.

_____

_____

_____

_____

_____

_____

GO ON →

3 Explain how the two folktales and the informational article are all helpful for someone who must write an original folktale. Support your answer with details from the article and the folktales.

_____

_____

_____

_____

_____

Directions for Part 2

You will now look at the two folktales and the informational article, take notes, and plan, draft, revise, and edit your original folktale. First read your assignment and the information about how your folktale will be scored. Then begin your work.

Your assignment:

The two stories you read are examples of typical folktales. Write your own folktale that is several paragraphs long and includes the characteristics of folktales that are discussed in the informational article and are shown in the stories you read. Make sure to include narrative elements such as dialogue, descriptions, characters, plot, setting, and a good ending. Develop your story completely.

REMEMBER: A well-written folktale:

- explains something about the world or teaches an important lesson
- relates to the beliefs and customs of a culture
- may include magic
- is well-organized and has a beginning, middle, and end
- uses transitions and a logical sequence of events
- uses details from the sources about folktales
- develops ideas fully
- uses clear language
- follows rules of writing (spelling, punctuation, and grammar)

GO ON →

Now begin work on your folktale. Manage your time carefully so that you can

1. plan your folktale

2. write your folktale

3. revise and edit the final draft of your folktale

For Part 2, you are being asked to write an original folktale that is several paragraphs long. Write your response on a separate sheet of paper. Remember to check your notes and your prewriting/planning as you write and then revise and edit your folktale.

Narrative 2

Student Directions

Task:

Your class is learning about the U.S. government. You have been chosen to write a narrative about the President of the United States. Before you decide what you will focus on, you do some research and find two articles that provide information about where the President lives and what the President does every day.

After you have looked at these sources, you will answer some questions about them. Briefly scan the sources and the three questions that follow. Then, go back and read the sources carefully to gain the information you will need to answer the questions and write a narrative about the President.

In Part 2, you will write a narrative using information you have read.

Directions for Part 1

You will now look at two sources. You can look at either of the sources as often as you like.

Research Questions:

After looking at the sources, use the rest of the time in Part 1 to answer three questions about them. Your answers to these questions will be scored. Also, your answers will help you think about the information you have read, which should help you write your narrative.

You may refer to the sources when you think it would be helpful. You may also look at your notes. Answer the questions in the space provided.

GO ON →

The White House: Our President's Home

The White House has been home to the President of the United States since 1800. President John Adams and his wife, Abigail, were the first people to ever live in it. President Theodore Roosevelt gave the house its name. In 1901, he had "The White House" put on his stationery, and ever since, the name has stuck.

The White House is a very large building that sits on about 18 acres of land. There is a main residence, an East Wing, and a West Wing. The White House has four main stories that are above ground. It also has a basement and even a floor below the basement. The entire house has a total of 132 rooms and 35 bathrooms!

The famous Oval Office, which is the President's official office, is in the West Wing. There are also many staff offices and meeting rooms in the West Wing. This is the section of the White House where the President does much of his work.

The East Wing has offices for the First Lady, who is the President's wife, and her staff. It also has a family theater and a garden room. When visitors go to tour the White House, they enter the house through an entrance in the East Wing.

The first floor of the main residence is where formal events are held. The second floor is where the President and his family's bedrooms are. There are also some guest bedrooms and private family rooms on this level. The third level of the White House residence is where the President's family goes to unwind. On this floor you will find a music room, a game room, a workout room, and a sun room. This is the area of the house where the most important family in the United States can simply relax.

GO ON →

Being President

(It's a Tough Job, but Someone's Got to Do It)

The President of the United States is one of the most powerful people on Earth. He is in charge of leading our country, but he also works with other nations to do what is best for people all over the world. He has a very important job. So far, only men have held this job, but someday soon a woman may serve.

In many ways, the President is a normal person like you or me. He gets up early at the White House, spends some time with his family, perhaps enjoys a good workout, and then goes off to work.

It is when he enters the Oval Office that he is no longer like everybody else. The President spends part of his day reading reports. He may discuss a new bill that he wants to sign into a law. He also hears about events that might have happened overnight. He needs to make sure he knows what is happening, not only here in our country, but all over the world. He will also spend some time reading letters that the public has sent him. These letters help him understand how people around the country feel about different topics.

The President might also meet with important people at the White House. Sometimes, an event will take place during the day that will cause the President to want to speak to the people. He may want to inform them of the event and what he thinks about it. He will have his staff announce that he will give a speech or hold a press conference at the White House to address the country.

Traveling all over the world is also a big part of what the President must do. He does not travel every day, but he travels often. He visits leaders of other nations. He might also travel to areas of the world that have been affected by a tragic event to show his support. All in all, the President is a very busy person with a very difficult job!

GO ON →

Research Questions

1 Explain how both sources could be used to describe the job of the U.S. President. Provide at least one piece of evidence from each source to support your answer.

_____

_____

_____

_____

_____

_____

2 Which main idea is supported by both sources?

(A) The White House is a home for the American public.

(B) The President rarely has time to rest at the White House.

(C) The White House has two floors below ground.

(D) The President's job is closely connected to the White House.

GO ON →

3 Which source would be more helpful in supporting the idea that the President has a very different type of job compared with the rest of the people in the country? Provide at least two pieces of evidence from the source to support your answer.

_____

_____

_____

_____

_____

GO ON →

Directions for Part 2

You will now look at your sources, take notes, and plan, draft, revise, and edit your narrative. First read your assignment and the information about how your narrative will be scored. Then begin your work.

Your assignment:

Your teacher wants you to write a narrative about the President of the United States. Write a narrative that is several paragraphs long from the point of view of the President. Explain a day in your life. Describe where you go in the White House and what you do during the day. Your narrative will be read by other students and the teacher. Make sure to organize the narrative well and to support your topic with details from the sources using your own words. Develop your ideas clearly.

REMEMBER: A well-written narrative:

- is well-organized and has a logical sequence of events
- has a beginning, middle, and end
- uses transitions
- uses details from the sources to support the topic
- develops ideas fully
- uses clear language
- follows rules of writing (spelling, punctuation, and grammar)

GO ON →

Now begin work on your narrative. Manage your time carefully so that you can

1. plan your narrative

2. write your narrative

3. revise and edit the final draft of your narrative

For Part 2, you are being asked to write a narrative that is several paragraphs long. Write your response on a separate sheet of paper. Remember to check your notes and your prewriting/planning as you write and then revise and edit your narrative.

Opinion 1

Student Directions

Task:

Bike sharing programs provide bicycles for a charge in cities. People pick up a bicycle at one "station" in the city. They use it to travel around the city. Then when they are done they return it to any other station in the same city.

For this task, you will be writing an opinion article related to the topic of bike sharing. Before you write your article, you will review three sources that provide an introduction to the topic and give two different viewpoints about whether bike sharing is a good idea.

After you have reviewed these sources, you will answer some questions about them. Briefly scan the sources and the three questions that follow. Then, go back and read the sources carefully to gain the information you will need to answer the questions and write an article.

In Part 2, you will write an opinion article using information you have read.

Directions for Part 1

You will now read several sources. You can look back at any of the sources as often as you like.

Research Questions:

After reading the sources, use the rest of the time in Part 1 to answer three questions about them. Your answers to these questions will be scored. Also, your answers will help you think about the information and ideas you have read, which should help you write your opinion article.

You may refer to the sources when you think it would be helpful. You may also look at your notes. Answer the questions in the space provided.

GO ON →

Bike Sharing Programs

Bike sharing programs allow people within a city to use bikes for a fee. People in Europe have been using bike sharing programs for years. Bike sharing stations have started to pop up in many of our own cities, too. This creative idea has been spreading across the country over the past few years. At the beginning of 2013, there were 22 programs running in American cities. Because the idea is so popular, people think that the number of programs will double very soon. These cities have other types of public transportation, too, such as subways and buses.

Bike sharing programs were started so that people would be able to use a bike easily when they needed one. The programs give people the option to use bikes to travel short distances around a big city. There are many bike stations that are set up in the city. People take a bike out of one station, use it for some time, and then return it to another station within the city.

People can use the bikes on any day and at any time. All of the stations are self-service stations. Each "dock," or area that holds the bikes, has an electronic machine. This machine takes payment from the customer and releases one of the bikes. The machine also starts to track the time that the bike is being used. The machine at the dock where the bike is returned can then calculate the total time the bike was in use.

Many people are using the bicycles in these programs. And cities are welcoming the stations. These are signs that bike sharing programs are a success.

GO ON →

Bike Sharing: A Great Idea

New and exciting programs have started in many cities: bike sharing programs. These innovative programs allow people to borrow and use bikes for a small price. They are a wonderful idea for many reasons.

When you decide to ride a bike to get somewhere instead of driving a car, that decision brings positive changes. One change that happens is that it takes a car off the road. This helps in a few ways. For one thing, it reduces traffic. If more people decided to ride a bike to get to and from work every day, fewer cars would be on the road at the same time. Rush hour traffic might not be that bad if this happened. It also helps to get rid of some of the pollution that cars produce. Over time, having fewer cars on city streets would help the environment greatly. Just think how much cleaner the air would be if this program were successful in all the major cities in the United States!

Bike sharing is also convenient for many of us. People living in a big city might not want to buy their own bicycles. Bikes can be expensive. They are also not easy to store in a small apartment. Unfortunately, bikes often are a target to be stolen. The bike sharing program is a great way to avoid all of these problems. The cost to use the bikes in these programs is low. When you are finished using the bike, you drop the bike off at a docking station. Where you will store the bike is not a problem. Also, if you don't own the bike, you won't worry about it being stolen after you have dropped it off.

Riding a bicycle is great exercise. Even short bike trips can help people live a healthier lifestyle. Bike sharing programs make it easier for busy people to be more active. These programs also create jobs. When a bike needs to be fixed, someone will need to fix it. Who will be there to answer any questions the public may have about the programs? People will need to be hired to do these tasks. Because the programs have become so successful, hundreds of jobs have already been created. As the programs spread to other cities, the number of available jobs will increase.

Bike sharing programs add so much value to the city and the people who live and work there. More and more cities are seeing the benefits. Many of them are making plans to start a bike sharing program. It is even possible that we may one day see these wonderful programs in every large city across America!

GO ON →

Bike Sharing: In Need of Repair

Bike sharing involves the use of bikes in a city for a fee. People pick up a bike at a bike docking station and then return it later to any station in the city. The number of cities with bike sharing programs continues to grow. Some of the larger cities have thousands of bikes and hundreds of stations as part of their program. At first, this sounds like a great idea, but unexpected problems have come up. Not everyone sees these programs as a good solution. They were designed to make life easier, but they have actually been causing some big headaches.

First of all, the bike docking stations are self-service, allowing people to use the bikes at any time. This means that an employee is not present at any of the stations. If something does not work properly when you try to take out a bike, nobody is there to help. This has been known to happen quite often. You can try to pay again and see if the bike will unlock the second time. You can also just leave the bike and lose your money. Calling customer service is another option, but that will take time. One of the hopes for these stations is that people will start using bicycles instead of other forms of transportation. If you need to be somewhere at a certain time, waiting to speak to a customer service representative to fix the problem is not something you would want to do. It is certainly easy to see how frustrating this can become.

Secondly, think about the space one or two bicycles take up. Then imagine thousands of them on already-crowded streets and sidewalks. That crowded picture in your head is a reality. These bikes are sitting on the street so that the public can access them. They are sitting in front of stores and apartment buildings where people live. Some docking stations hold up to 50 or 60 bicycles. These docks are taking up a lot of valuable space all over the city.

Finally, if you have ever walked around busy city streets, you know that you need to be alert. You need to watch for cars and buses, and you need to be careful not to bump into anyone walking beside you. Now, add thousands of people on bicycles. This can be a dangerous situation. The people riding the bikes may not always be experienced bike riders, either. As a result, someone could get seriously hurt.

GO ON →

The overall idea of the bike sharing program may be a good one. Is it worth the problems it creates, though? If people want to use a bike to get around, they have options. They can either buy their own or rent one from a bike store. Having a bike sharing program as a third option is simply not necessary.

Research Questions

1 Which detail from the first article is NOT important in helping to explain how bike sharing works?

(A) Bike sharing programs allow offer city bikes for a fee.

(B) Cities also offer public transportation such as buses.

(C) People can use the city bikes whenever they want.

(D) These programs appear to be popular in cities.

2 What is one advantage of bike sharing? What is one disadvantage? Provide specific reasons from at least two sources in your answer. Be sure to name each source.

_____

_____

_____

_____

_____

GO ON →

3 Why do you think it is difficult for people to agree about the topic of bike sharing? Explain why and support your answer with at least two details from the sources.

_____

_____

_____

_____

_____

Copyright © McGraw-Hill Education

GO ON →

Grade 4 • **Performance-Based Tasks**

Directions for Part 2

You will now look at your sources, take notes, and plan, draft, revise, and edit your article. First read your assignment and the information about how your opinion article will be scored. Then begin your work.

Your assignment:

Your community may be starting a bike sharing program soon. Write an article that is several paragraphs long for your community newspaper in which you give your opinion about this idea. Your article will be read by the parents and students in your community. Make sure to state your opinion clearly and to support your opinion with reasons from the sources using your own words. Develop your ideas clearly.

REMEMBER: A well-written opinion article:

- expresses a clear opinion
- is well-organized and stays on the topic
- has an introduction and conclusion
- uses transitions
- uses details from the sources to support the opinion
- develops ideas fully
- uses clear language
- follows rules of writing (spelling, punctuation, and grammar)

GO ON →

Now begin work on your opinion article. Manage your time carefully so that you can

1. plan your article
2. write your article
3. revise and edit the final draft of your article

For Part 2, you are being asked to write an article that is several paragraphs long. Write your response on a separate sheet of paper. Remember to check your notes and your prewriting/planning as you write and then revise and edit your article.

Opinion 2

Student Directions

Task:

Many students play sports after school. For some kids this is their favorite thing to do. But how do these sports affect how students do in school? Should students have to get good grades in order to be allowed to play sports in the first place?

For this task, you will be writing an opinion article related to the topic of getting good grades in order to play sports. Before you write your article, you will review three sources that provide an introduction to after-school sports and give two different viewpoints about whether good grades should be necessary to play sports.

After you have reviewed these sources, you will answer some questions about them. Briefly scan the sources and the three questions that follow. Then, go back and read the sources carefully to gain the information you will need to answer the questions and write an article.

In Part 2, you will write an opinion article using information that you have read.

Directions for Part 1

You will now read several sources. You can look back at any of the sources as often as you like.

Research Questions:

After reading the sources, use the rest of the time in Part 1 to answer three questions about them. Your answers to these questions will be scored. Also, your answers will help you think about the information and ideas you have read, which should help you write your opinion article.

You may refer to the sources when you think it would be helpful. You may also look at your notes. Answer the questions in the space provided.

GO ON →

Kids and After-School Sports

After-school sports are a part of life for many students around the country. In elementary school, these sports could range from soccer to baseball and softball. Some schools offer football and basketball, too. The sports programs support the physical education that students receive at school.

Students practice their skills as a team. The practices may occur one or more days after school during the week. Students may put in one to four or five hours in practice time each week. They may also have games with other teams. Usually the practices are during the week and the games are on the weekends. The schedule is different for every school, though.

Many boys and girls enjoy being in after-school sports and look forward to their practices. The sports are good for them, too. Students remain active and learn to work together as a team. In fact, many students love the experience so much that they continue playing the sport through middle school and high school.

Although sports are a lot of fun, schoolwork should always come first in a student's life. Students should not spend less time on their homework and projects after school just because they are playing a sport. Parents need to make sure that they help students balance their schoolwork and their sport. Students should always continue to work hard on getting good grades.

After-school sports can be a lot of fun and are a good way to stay active. They also teach students how to work with others as a team. But students must remember that their education should always be more important than any sport they play after school.

GO ON →

Grades Come First!

After-school sports are available at many elementary schools. Students love to join these sports to have fun and make new friends. But the sports can easily take up too much time in a student's life. There are practices up to a few times a week, and then there are games on weekends. Students also practice at home to improve their skills. All of this takes time away from more important things like studying for tests. For this reason, students must be required to get good grades in order to play a sport after school.

Schools were not created to train athletes. Their main goal is to educate. Schools that provide an optional sport should do so only if the student is able to handle schoolwork as well. The only way to know this is by looking at the student's grades. A student who is doing well and succeeding in all subject areas should be able to take on a sport after school. That student can likely handle the responsibility and manage his or her time so that schoolwork does not become less important. But if a student needs to improve scores in one or more subject areas, it does not make sense to allow that student to take time away from schoolwork by joining a sport. It would mean having less time to study due to all the practices and games.

Allowing any student to play an after-school sport regardless of grades suggests that schoolwork is not as important as sports. This is simply not true. Obviously, schools know that education is very important. That is why schools need to require good grades to play sports. This will help parents and students understand that learning comes first.

After-school sports should be viewed as a reward for working hard and succeeding in school. Students who want to play a sport must work to get the grades needed. This will motivate them to try harder in school. The hard work and dedication will then transfer to the sport. Once students are accepted into an after-school sport, they will already know what it is like to set a goal and achieve it. They will have learned lessons that they can apply to being a team player.

It may be difficult to turn down some students because their grades are not high enough; however, schools must remember that their most important goal is to teach kids. Using after-school sports as a reward for getting good grades will help schools achieve that goal. And along the way, kids will learn a lot more than just reading and writing.

GO ON →

Grades Come First!

After-school sports are available at many elementary schools. Students love to join these sports to have fun and make new friends. But the sports can easily take up too much time in a student's life. There are practices up to a few times a week, and then there are games on weekends. Students also practice at home to improve their skills. All of this takes time away from more important things like studying for tests. For this reason, students must be required to get good grades in order to play a sport after school.

Schools were not created to train athletes. Their main goal is to educate. Schools that provide an optional sport should do so only if the student is able to handle schoolwork as well. The only way to know this is by looking at the student's grades. A student who is doing well and succeeding in all subject areas should be able to take on a sport after school. That student can likely handle the responsibility and manage his or her time so that schoolwork does not become less important. But if a student needs to improve scores in one or more subject areas, it does not make sense to allow that student to take time away from schoolwork by joining a sport. It would mean having less time to study due to all the practices and games.

Allowing any student to play an after-school sport regardless of grades suggests that schoolwork is not as important as sports. This is simply not true. Obviously, schools know that education is very important. That is why schools need to require good grades to play sports. This will help parents and students understand that learning comes first.

After-school sports should be viewed as a reward for working hard and succeeding in school. Students who want to play a sport must work to get the grades needed. This will motivate them to try harder in school. The hard work and dedication will then transfer to the sport. Once students are accepted into an after-school sport, they will already know what it is like to set a goal and achieve it. They will have learned lessons that they can apply to being a team player.

It may be difficult to turn down some students because their grades are not high enough; however, schools must remember that their most important goal is to teach kids. Using after-school sports as a reward for getting good grades will help schools achieve that goal. And along the way, kids will learn a lot more than just reading and writing.

GO ON →

Sports Are Separate from School

Some schools have decided that students cannot play sports after school if they do not get good grades. This is unfair. Students should not be stopped from playing sports based on how well they can read, write, or do math. Schoolwork is most important for a student, but sports are not related to it.

This is a "hot topic" that people are talking about all over the country. They have different opinions. They have even done research that studies the relationship between getting good grades in school and playing a sport after school. One study found that playing a sport did not have a bad effect on a student's grades. It found that playing a sport sometimes even caused a student to get better grades. This supports the idea that students should not have to get good grades to play.

"How can playing a sport improve my grades?" you may ask. The answer has to do with the ideas behind playing a sport. It teaches you to be responsible and to practice. You learn to set goals and work hard to achieve them. This type of self-discipline is helpful in the classroom, too. It can help you study harder and finish your homework even when you feel like doing something else. The coach of the team can help you push yourself to do better on and off the field.

Playing a sport also has other benefits. Sports help to keep students active and healthy. Students learn about teamwork, and they make new friends with the same interests. Sports also teach students to be responsible in all parts of their lives. Every student should be allowed to have these benefits, not just the students who get good grades.

Many schools have created policies related to after-school sports. They have decided that students must have a certain grade point average or they must score a certain number on tests to be able to play in a sport after school. This does not make sense. Students learn in different ways. Some students learn certain subjects more easily than other students. Is it fair to punish a student because he or she did not score a few points higher on a test? What kind of message does this send to students and their parents? These policies do not help students improve their grades. They only make students feel like they are not good enough.

GO ON →

The main problem with connecting good grades to sports, though, is that schools are deciding which students get to play and which do not. After-school sports should be open to everyone. Parents and families should decide whether a child can play a sport, not the school. Sports are fun activities that take place outside the classroom. They have nothing to do with what happens inside the classroom.

GO ON →

Research Questions

1 Which sentence from the first source supports the opinion of the second and third sources?

(A) Usually the practices are during the week and the games are on the weekends.

(B) In fact, many students love the experience so much that they continue playing the sport through middle school and high school.

(C) Although sports are a lot of fun, schoolwork should always come first in a student's life.

(D) They also teach students how to work with others as a team.

2 Why does the author of the third source ask the reader questions? Explain how the author uses these questions to support the opinion in the source.

_____

_____

_____

_____

_____

GO ON →

Grade 4 • Performance-Based Tasks

Name: _____ Date: _____

3 Which source supports the author's opinion better: the second
source or the third source? Explain why, supporting your answer
with at least two details from the source.

_____

_____

_____

_____

_____

GO ON →

Directions for Part 2

You will now look at your sources, take notes, and plan, draft, revise, and edit your article. First read your assignment and the information about how your opinion article will be scored. Then begin your work.

Your assignment:

Your school may soon start requiring that students get good grades in order to play sports after school. Write an article that is several paragraphs long for your school newspaper in which you give your opinion about this idea. Your article will be read by parents and the students and teachers in your school. Make sure to state your opinion clearly and to support your opinion with reasons from the sources using your own words. Develop your ideas clearly.

REMEMBER: A well-written opinion article:

- expresses a clear opinion
- is well-organized and stays on the topic
- has an introduction and conclusion
- uses transitions
- uses details from the sources to support the opinion
- develops ideas fully
- uses clear language
- follows rules of writing (spelling, punctuation, and grammar)

GO ON →

Now begin work on your opinion article. Manage your time carefully so that you can

1. plan your article

2. write your article

3. revise and edit the final draft of your article

For Part 2, you are being asked to write an article that is several paragraphs long. Write your response on a separate sheet of paper. Remember to check your notes and your prewriting/planning as you write and then revise and edit your article.

Informational

Student Directions

Task:

Your after-school music club is creating a newsletter about famous musicians in history. Each member must write an article about a different musician. You have decided to write about Ella Fitzgerald, a famous jazz singer. You do some research and find two articles that provide information about Ella Fitzgerald and her contributions to jazz music.

After you have looked at these sources, you will answer some questions about them. Briefly scan the sources and the three questions that follow. Then, go back and read the sources carefully to gain the information you will need to answer the questions and write an informational article.

In Part 2, you will write an informational article using information you have read.

Directions for Part 1

You will now look at two sources. You can look at either of the sources as often as you like.

Research Questions:

After looking at the sources, use the rest of the time in Part 1 to answer three questions about them. Your answers to these questions will be scored. Also, your answers will help you think about the information you have read, which should help you write your informational article.

You may refer to the sources when you think it would be helpful. You may also look at your notes. Answer the questions in the space provided.

GO ON →

Just Stand There and Sing

The year was 1934. A shy teenager stood on the stage of the Apollo Theater in Harlem, a neighborhood of New York City. She was competing in a talent contest called Amateur Night. The crowd laughed at her and yelled, "Boo!" But then she opened her mouth and started to sing, and soon the crowd fell silent. As she finished the song, the audience burst into applause and demanded another song. That night she left the theater with the first-place prize.

That evening at the Apollo was the beginning of Ella Fitzgerald's legendary career as a jazz singer. Amazingly, Ella did not even plan to sing that night. She had entered the contest as a dancer, but she felt she could not beat one of the dancing acts before her. So, at the last minute, she decided to sing instead.

Ella Jane Fitzgerald was born on April 25, 1917, in Newport News, Virginia. Early in her childhood, she moved with her mother, Tempie, and her stepfather to Yonkers, New York. Later, after Tempie's death, Ella lived with her aunt, Virginia Williams, in Harlem. She had a tough time in Harlem. Her grades fell in school, and she got into a lot of trouble. There was little money to go around.

Amateur Night at the Apollo was the turning point in Ella's life. She entered, and won, more singing contests. In 1935, she began singing with famous jazz drummer Chick Webb and his band. They often played at the Savoy Ballroom in Harlem. At the Savoy, large jazz bands played a type of music called swing, and people danced through the night. The Savoy was nicknamed "the home of happy feet."

In 1938, when Ella was 21 years old, she recorded a song called "A-Tisket, A-Tasket." This was the song that made her famous. The album sold a million copies, and the song was a number-one hit.

In 1939, Chick Webb died, and Ella took over as leader of his band. Her career took off. After a couple of years as bandleader, she became a solo artist. Over the next 50 years, Ella recorded more than 200 albums and toured around the world. She worked with just about every great jazz and pop artist

GO ON →

of her time: Louis Armstrong, Duke Ellington, Frank Sinatra, and many more. Ella also sang on television shows, such as *The Tonight Show* and *The Nat King Cole Show*.

Ella became a great performer, even though she was a shy, humble, and private person off the stage. "I know I'm no glamour girl," she said, "and it's not easy for me to get up in front of a crowd of people. It used to bother me a lot, but now . . . I just stand there and sing."

Ella Fitzgerald was incredibly successful. She was the top female jazz singer in the United States for over half a century. She won 13 Grammy Awards, sold 40 million albums in her lifetime, and performed 26 times at New York's world-famous Carnegie Hall. In 1987, President Ronald Reagan awarded her the National Medal of Arts.

In 1991, at Carnegie Hall, Ella gave her last concert. It was a special conclusion to a historic career. She sang perfectly her final night on stage, and the audience roared with appreciation. Five years later, in 1996, Ella died in her California home.

Source #2

Ella Lives On

It takes a lot of talent to earn the nickname the "First Lady of Song." Jazz singer Ella Fitzgerald had all that talent and then some. It is impossible to measure the influence that Ella has had even after her death in 1996. She lives on in the memories and hearts of music lovers around the world.

Ella's greatest legacy is her music. This is the gift she gave to the world. People still buy and listen to her recordings every day. She is a hero to countless singers. Ella's music still wins over new jazz fans all the time.

In Newport News, Virginia, Ella's hometown, people are making sure to remember her. The Ella Fitzgerald Theater opened there in 2008. In 2013, Newport News hosted its 15th annual Ella Fitzgerald Music Festival. This festival includes a show where various artists sing Ella's music as a tribute to her.

In 2007, the United States Postal Service honored Ella in a different way. It made a special stamp with her face on it. That same year, a group of well-known singers released a disc called *We All Love Ella*.

Ella also lives on through the Ella Fitzgerald Charitable Foundation. She started this group before her death. It gives money to support children in need and to spread the love of music. When Ella was alive, she cared deeply about children from poor families. She once said, "It isn't where you came from, it's where you're going that counts."

GO ON →

Research Questions

1 Which information is found in both sources?

   Ⓐ when Ella was discovered as a singer

   Ⓑ what town Ella was born in

   Ⓒ how Ella felt about singing in front of others

   Ⓓ why Ella sang with Chick Webb

2 During your review of the sources, you learn that Ella was well-loved by many people around the world. Provide at least one piece of evidence from each source to support this claim.

_____

_____

_____

_____

_____

GO ON →

3 Which source does a better job of explaining Ella's influence in jazz music? Provide three pieces of evidence from the source to support your answer.

_____

_____

_____

_____

_____

_____

GO ON →

Directions for Part 2

You will now look at your sources, take notes, and plan, draft, revise, and edit your article. First read your assignment and the information about how your informational article will be scored. Then begin your work.

Your assignment:

Your music club is putting together a newsletter about famous musicians of the past. Write an article that is several paragraphs long in which you explain why Ella Fitzgerald is important to the history of jazz. Your article will be read by the other students in your club and by parents. Make sure to have a main idea, to organize your article logically, and to support your main idea with details from the sources using your own words. Develop your ideas clearly.

REMEMBER: A well-written informational article:

- has a clear main idea
- is well-organized and stays on the topic
- has an introduction and conclusion
- uses transitions
- uses details from the sources to support the main idea
- develops ideas fully
- uses clear language
- follows rules of writing (spelling, punctuation, and grammar)

GO ON →

Now begin work on your informational article. Manage your time carefully so that you can

1. plan your article

2. write your article

3. revise and edit the final draft of your article

For Part 2, you are being asked to write an article that is several paragraphs long. Write your response on a separate sheet of paper. Remember to check your notes and your prewriting/planning as you write and then revise and edit your article.

Make It Work

1   "I like to do many different things," Ruthie explained to Rita one day. "So what I do is plan four different ways that the day can go. That way, I'm ready for anything." Rita and Ruthie were twin sisters, but their approach to planning their days was completely different.

2   Ruthie could not understand why Rita had the same routine every single day. When Rita got home from school, she first had a snack of an apple and peanut butter. Next, she changed out of her school clothes. After that she set her notebook and assignments on the dining room table. She finished each assignment in order by subject. When she was finished, only then would she go out to play or hang out with her friends. After that, Rita would have dinner with the family, help with the dishes, and read until bedtime. "That way," Rita explained, "everything feels calm and orderly. That makes me feel like I can accomplish any task."

3   Ruthie, on the other hand, preferred to put her social activities first. Her friend Micah might ask her to join a kickball game after school, and so if that happened, Ruthie would do that. After the game, Ruthie would come home— she would be too late for a snack—and have dinner with the family, help with the dishes, and then do her homework before bed.

4   That was Plan A. Plan B occurred if her friend Josie invited her to sing with her band. This was something Josie did in the evenings after dinner in her family's garage. On band day, Ruthie did her homework after school. That is, Ruthie did homework after school only if Derek didn't want to play computer games at his house. If she went to Derek's, then it was Plan C, because Derek's parents would always invite Ruthie to stay for dinner.

5   "And then there is Plan S," Ruthie explained.

6   "What is Plan S?" Rita asked.

7   "S is for Surprise," Ruthie said. Rita looked at her sister and laughed.

8   "I guess everyone is different," Rita said. "We each get our homework done, eat right, and do our chores. So I guess no one can complain!"

GO ON →

1 **Part A:** What is a synonym of the word **routine** as it is used in paragraph 2 of the story?

Ⓐ system

Ⓑ creation

Ⓒ product

Ⓓ disorder

Part B: Draw a line to match the following parts of Rita's routine with the order in which they occur.

First		Plays with friends
Second		Has a snack
Third		Helps with the dishes

2 **Part A:** What is the theme of the story?

Ⓐ There is usually only one right way to do a job.

Ⓑ Work should always come before play.

Ⓒ People may not have the same interests or ways of doing things.

Ⓓ Making plans is fun, but most people don't stick to them.

Part B: Which sentence from paragraph 1 **best** supports the theme? Underline the sentence.

> "I like to do many different things," Ruthie explained to Rita one day. "So what I do is plan four different ways that the day can go. That way, I'm ready for anything." Rita and Ruthie were twin sisters, but their approach to planning their days was completely different.

GO ON →

3 **Part A:** Which word below describes Rita's character?

(A) curious

(B) uninterested

(C) organized

(D) fearful

Part B: Which sentence from the story **best** supports the answer you selected in Part A?

(A) "Next, she changed out of her school clothes." (Paragraph 2)

(B) "She finished each assignment in order by subject." (Paragraph 2)

(C) "Rita looked at her sister and laughed." (Paragraph 7)

(D) "'I guess everyone is different,' Rita said." (Paragraph 8)

GO ON →

4 **Part A:** Which word below describes Ruthie's character?

(A) kind

(B) disorganized

(C) lazy

(D) unpredictable

Part B: Which **two** sentences from the story support the answer you selected in Part A?

(A) "'I like to do many different things,' Ruthie explained to Rita one day." (Paragraph 1)

(B) "Ruthie could not understand why Rita had the same routine every single day." (Paragraph 2)

(C) "Ruthie, on the other hand, preferred to put her social activities first." (Paragraph 3)

(D) "This was something Josie did in the evenings after dinner in her family's garage." (Paragraph 4)

(E) "On band day, Ruthie did her homework after school." (Paragraph 4)

(F) "If she went to Derek's, then it was Plan C, because Derek's parents would always invite Ruthie to stay for dinner." (Paragraph 4)

GO ON →

5 **Part A:** What makes Ruthie's daily routine different from Rita's?

(A) Ruthie plans each day well ahead of time, and Rita changes each day.

(B) Rita does homework at the same time each day, and Ruthie does not.

(C) Ruthie sometimes helps with dishes, but Rita always does.

(D) Rita is involved in four or five different activities, but Ruthie is involved in only two.

Part B: Which sentence from the story **best** supports the statement in Part A?

(A) "When she was finished, only then would she go out to play or hang out with her friends." (Paragraph 2)

(B) "Her friend Micah might ask her to join a kickball game after school, and so if that happened, Ruthie would do that." (Paragraph 3)

(C) "Plan B occurred if her friend Josie invited her to sing with her band." (Paragraph 4)

(D) "That is, Ruthie did homework after school only if Derek didn't want to play computer games at his house." (Paragraph 4)

GO ON →

Read "A Man of His Word" and answer the questions that follow.

A Man of His Word

1   Long ago, a poor farmer named Weston went off to another land in search of work. He was offered a job as a servant to a master who agreed to pay him six pieces of silver for a year's work. However, he would not give Weston any wages until the end of the year. Weston agreed to trust the rich man, for what choice did he have?

2   At the year's end, Weston wanted to return to his family. The rich man said, "Weston, you have been a fine servant, and I have your wages. However, I have something more valuable to offer you instead of your wages. I will not tell you yet what it is. Will you trust me and take that, or will you take your six pieces of silver?" Weston, who trusted his master, took the risk.

3   The master said, "What I have to offer you is three pieces of advice. First, never take a shortcut when you can take a main road. Second, never accept an offer when you are not in need. Third, honesty is the best policy." The master then produced one silver coin to be used for Weston's journey home and handed Weston two cakes. "Here is one cake for your journey. This second cake wrapped in cloth is not to be eaten until you get home, and you must share it with your family." Weston agreed to follow his master's advice and headed off, wondering if he had made the right choice. However, his master had always been good to him, and Weston knew he could trust him.

4   Along the road, Weston met two peddlers who suggested they all take a shortcut through the woods to the inn. It would save at least two miles of walking and would get them to the inn before darkness fell. But Weston remembered his master's first piece of advice and declined their invitation. "I think I'll stick to the main road," he said. "I'll see you there."

5   When Weston arrived at the inn, a man in a cloak was just leaving. "Young man," said the stranger, in a hurried whisper. "Although I have already paid for my room, I have decided to leave. You are welcome to the room." Weston looked at the stranger and the room key that the stranger held out to him and then remembered his master's second piece of advice. While a free room would be nice, Weston knew he had one piece of silver and was not in need.

GO ON →

Copyright © McGraw-Hill Education

6   Instead of using the key himself, Weston brought it to the innkeeper. "You can take the room, for it's the last one I have," offered the innkeeper. Just then, the two peddlers came in, their shirts torn. They had been robbed in the woods! Hearing of the free room, they decided to take it. Weston was happy to sleep in the stable, and he ate his first cake for his meal.

7   That night a sheriff arrived at the inn looking for a stolen box of jewels. While searching the peddlers' room, the sheriff found the box, but it was empty. The peddlers knew nothing about the jewels. Just then the innkeeper remembered Weston sleeping in the stable. Weston told the sheriff of the man and the key. With that information, the sheriff freed the peddlers and set off to find the stranger. Weston realized that if he had taken that room, he might have been accused of the crime.

8   When Weston arrived home at long last, his wife and children hugged him in welcome. In addition, they had a surprise. They showed him a bag of money they had found on the road to town. After their years of poverty, here was a reward!

9   Weston thought about his master's third piece of advice and told his family, "We must be honest and try to find the owner." His family began to protest when there was a knock at the door.

10   An old woman stood before him and asked, "Young man, can you help me? I have lost my bag of money, all I have in the world!" Weston's wife agreed they must return the money. The old woman cried out in joy. From the bag the grateful woman removed a gold coin and pressed it into Weston's hand. "Thank you for your honesty. May you have prosperity!" Weston silently hoped that the woman was right, that the gold coin marked the beginning of the end of the family's poverty.

11   As the family sat down to their small meal, they talked about how to spend the reward. Weston then brought out the second cake for them to share. When he broke the cake in two, out of one side fell six pieces of silver, his wages! And out of the second half fell six pieces of gold. Weston realized that the disguise of the cake was to save him from getting robbed. By following his master's advice and instructions, Weston was rewarded with a safe return, money for his family, and the satisfaction that he, himself, was a man who kept his promise.

GO ON →

6 **Part A:** What does the word **prosperity** mean as it is used in paragraph 10 of the story?

(A) happiness

(B) sadness

(C) good fortune

(D) bad luck

Part B: Which phrase from paragraph 10 is a hint to the meaning of **prosperity**?

(A) "... all I have in the world!"

(B) "... must return the money."

(C) "... the grateful woman removed a gold coin ..."

(D) "... end of the family's poverty."

GO ON →

7 **Part A:** During the story, Weston has to make several choices. Which choice is most important to the plot of the story?

(A) He decides to leave his job to go home to his family.

(B) He trusts that his master will pay him at the end of the year.

(C) He accepts three pieces of advice as payment for his work.

(D) He sleeps in the stable at the inn instead of accepting a free room.

Part B: Which **two** pieces of text evidence support your answer in Part A?

(A) "Long ago, a poor farmer named Weston went off to another land in search of work." (Paragraph 1)

(B) "Weston agreed to trust the rich man, for what choice did he have?" (Paragraph 1)

(C) "However, I have something more valuable to offer you instead of your wages." (Paragraph 2)

(D) "I will not tell you yet what it is." (Paragraph 2)

(E) "The master then produced one silver coin to be used for Weston's journey home and handed Weston two cakes." (Paragraph 3)

(F) "Weston agreed to follow his master's advice and headed off, wondering if he had made the right choice." (Paragraph 3)

GO ON →

8 **Part A:** Why does Weston turn down the peddlers' offer to travel with them through the woods?

(A) Weston enjoys walking and wants to take his time.

(B) Weston is following his master's advice.

(C) Weston thinks the peddlers are dishonest.

(D) Weston thinks the shortcut might be unsafe.

Part B: What phrase from paragraph 3 supports your answer in Part A?

(A) "... never take a shortcut when you can take a main road."

(B) "... never accept an offer when you are not in need."

(C) "... honesty is the best policy."

(D) "... cake wrapped in cloth is not to be eaten ..."

GO ON →

Grade 4 • **End-of-Year Assessment**

9 **Part A:** What hint does the author give that the stranger in the cloak may have something to hide?

Ⓐ The stranger speaks in a hurried whisper.

Ⓑ The stranger holds out the key.

Ⓒ The innkeeper has no more rooms.

Ⓓ The innkeeper offers the stranger's room to Weston.

Part B: Underline the detail from paragraph 7 that shows why this hint about the stranger is important to the story.

That night a sheriff arrived at the inn looking for a stolen box of jewels. While searching the peddlers' room, the sheriff found the box, but it was empty. The peddlers knew nothing about the jewels. Just then the innkeeper remembered Weston sleeping in the stable. Weston told the sheriff of the man and the key. With that information, the sheriff freed the peddlers and set off to find the stranger. Weston realized that if he had taken that room, he might have been accused of the crime.

GO ON →

10 **Part A:** Which character trait below **best** describes the master?

(A) strict

(B) dishonest

(C) wise

(D) patient

Part B: Which detail from the story illustrates that character trait?

(A) The master hides Weston's wages in a cake so that he will not be robbed.

(B) The master tells Weston that he has been a fine servant.

(C) The master gives Weston enough time to make a good decision about whether to take his wages.

(D) The master gives Weston one piece of silver so that he can have a safe trip home.

GO ON →

11 **Part A:** Which of the following states a theme of the story?

(A) Trusting strangers will lead to trouble.

(B) It is important to be honest.

(C) Hard work is always rewarded.

(D) Think carefully before you decide to take advice.

Part B: Which event from the story supports your answer in Part A?

(A) The stranger leaves an empty jewel box in his room at the inn.

(B) The innkeeper tells the sheriff where to find Weston.

(C) The family shows Weston a bag of money they found on the road.

(D) The old woman gives Weston's family a piece of gold.

GO ON →

12 **Part A:** Which phrase below **best** describes Weston's character?

(A) angry and determined

(B) bashful and kind

(C) honest and dependable

(D) reckless and impatient

Part B: Which sentence from the story supports your answer?

(A) "When Weston arrived home at long last, his wife and children hugged him in welcome." (Paragraph 8)

(B) "Weston silently hoped that the woman was right, that the gold coin marked the beginning of the end of the family's poverty." (Paragraph 10)

(C) "As the family sat down to their small meal, they talked about how to spend the reward." (Paragraph 11)

(D) "Weston then brought out the second cake for them to share." (Paragraph 11)

GO ON →

13 Use the statements below to summarize the story. Number the
statements to show the order in which they occur. Select **only** those
statements that accurately describe what happens in the story.

A The master's advice saves Weston from being robbed
and from being accused of a crime as he travels home.

___

B Weston convinces his family to give a bag of money back
to a woman who lost it.

___

C Weston chooses to trust his master and take a payment
that is more valuable than his wages.

___

D Following the master's instructions leaves Weston with
money for his family and teaches him the importance
of keeping his word.

___

E The master offers to pay Weston six pieces of silver and
six pieces of gold at the end of one year.

___

F Weston receives three pieces of advice and some
instructions and agrees to follow them.

___

GO ON →

Mathew Brady, Photographer

1   The photographer Mathew Brady changed the way people depict war. Before Brady, artists often portrayed war as noble and heroic. The Civil War photographs taken by Brady and his team showed the harsh truth.

2   Mathew Brady was born around 1823. As a teenager he learned about the new art form of photography from his teacher, the inventor and artist Samuel Morse. By 1844 Brady had opened his own photography business. Soon, some of the most famous Americans of the day were having their pictures taken by Brady, such as former president John Tyler.

3   Brady suffered from poor eyesight for much of his life, yet he had a gift for posing people in ways that brought out who they truly were. Early in 1860, many believed that Abraham Lincoln was too awkward-looking to be elected president. On February 27 of that year, Brady took a photograph that changed people's minds. It brought out Lincoln's strength of character and made him look like a statesman. Later that day, Lincoln made a powerful speech at the Cooper Institute. Later that year, he was elected president. Looking back, Lincoln said, "Brady and the Cooper Institute made me president."

4   Brady found great success in photographing the rich and powerful. He wanted to take photography in a new direction, however. When the Civil War broke out in 1861, Brady created a "corps" of twenty photographers to document it. Back then, photography required heavy, expensive equipment, and each photographer on Brady's team needed a horse-drawn wagon. The thousands of photos these men took—which Brady took credit for—fully captured the destruction of battle. The idea that being a soldier was glamorous was gone forever. After seeing one exhibition, a *New York Times* reporter wrote, "The photos bring home to us the terrible reality ... of war."

5   Brady spent a fortune funding the Civil War photographs. He went broke when no one bought them. At the time, people wanted to forget the war. Sadly, Brady's business never recovered. He died penniless in 1896.

6   Mathew Brady had pioneered the use of photos to document important events. Today the photographs of Brady and his team are considered a treasured record of our past. The priceless photographs captured the nation during a crucial moment in history.

GO ON →

14 **Part A:** What does the word **priceless** mean as it is used in paragraph 6 of the article?

(A) low-priced

(B) half-finished

(C) extremely valuable

(D) extremely detailed

Part B: Which phrase from the article helps the reader understand the meaning of **priceless**?

(A) ". . . thousands of photos . . ." (Paragraph 4)

(B) ". . . wanted to forget . . ." (Paragraph 5)

(C) ". . . never recovered." (Paragraph 5)

(D) ". . . treasured record . . ." (Paragraph 6)

GO ON →

15 **Part A:** What problem did Mathew Brady help Abraham Lincoln solve?

(A) People did not have any idea of what Lincoln looked like.

(B) People thought Lincoln did not have the right appearance to be president.

(C) Lincoln needed to make a very important speech at the Cooper Institute.

(D) Lincoln needed to know what had taken place during the Civil War battles.

Part B: Which sentence from the article **best** supports the answer to Part A?

(A) "Early in 1860, many believed that Abraham Lincoln was too awkward-looking to be elected president." (Paragraph 3)

(B) "Later that day, Lincoln made a powerful speech at the Cooper Institute." (Paragraph 3)

(C) "Brady found great success in photographing the rich and powerful." (Paragraph 4)

(D) "The idea that being a soldier was glamorous was gone forever." (Paragraph 4)

GO ON →

16 **Part A:** What is a main idea of "Mathew Brady, Photographer"?

(A) Mathew Brady lost all his money after the Civil War.

(B) Mathew Brady learned about photography from Samuel Morse.

(C) Mathew Brady photographed John Tyler, a former president.

(D) Mathew Brady helped to show how destructive war can be.

Part B: Which **two** of the following provide details that support the main idea in Part A?

(A) "Before Brady, artists often portrayed war as noble and heroic." (Paragraph 1)

(B) "As a teenager he learned about the new art form of photography from his teacher, the inventor and artist Samuel Morse." (Paragraph 2)

(C) "Brady suffered from poor eyesight for much of his life, yet he had a gift for posing people in ways that brought out who they truly were." (Paragraph 3)

(D) "Back then, photography required heavy, expensive equipment, and each photographer on Brady's team needed a horse-drawn wagon." (Paragraph 4)

(E) "The thousands of photos these men took—which Brady took credit for—fully captured the destruction of battle." (Paragraph 4)

(F) "At the time, people wanted to forget the war." (Paragraph 5)

GO ON →

17 **Part A:** Arrange the events from the article in the order in which they occurred. Write the sentences in the correct order in the chart below.

| A Brady opens his photography business. |
| B Brady hires a team to photograph the Civil War. |
| C Brady meets Abraham Lincoln. |
| D Brady meets Samuel Morse. |

1	
2	
3	
4	

Part B: Which **two** phrases from paragraph 3 are evidence that the author used a chronological text structure?

(A) "... a gift for posing people ..."

(B) "Early in 1860 ..."

(C) "... to be elected president."

(D) "It brought out ..."

(E) "... at the Cooper Institute."

(F) "Later that year ..."

GO ON →

18 **Part A:** Which of the following claims is supported by the most relevant and sufficient evidence within "Mathew Brady, Photographer"?

(A) Brady was a father of photojournalism, the use of photos to tell news stories.

(B) Brady's poor eyesight ended up making him a more successful photographer.

(C) Brady believed that the Civil War was a mistake and should be ended quickly.

(D) Brady believed his greatest achievement was photographing Abraham Lincoln.

Part B: Which statement from the article is evidence that **best** supports your answer?

(A) "The Civil War photographs taken by Brady and his team showed the harsh truth." (Paragraph 1)

(B) "On February 27 of that year, Brady took a photograph that changed people's minds." (Paragraph 3)

(C) "Brady spent a fortune funding the Civil War photographs." (Paragraph 5)

(D) "Mathew Brady had pioneered the use of photos to document important events." (Paragraph 6)

GO ON →

Now you will read about the topic of food chains. The first text, "Food Chains," is an article, and the second text is a firsthand account, "Journal Entry for May 15." As you read the texts, pay close attention to details in the pieces. You will answer questions about both texts.

Read "Food Chains" and "Journal Entry for May 15" and answer the questions that follow.

Food Chains

1   Living things need energy to live and grow, but where do they get their energy? The answer is simple once you think about it. Living things get energy from food. The energy in food is passed from one organism to another in a food chain. Sunlight is how most food chains get started.

2   Food chains include producers, consumers, and decomposers. First, green plants are called producers in a food chain because they use the Sun's energy to produce their own food. Then animals consume plants and other animals since they cannot make their own food. Animals are called consumers on a food chain. Finally, decomposers on a food chain break down organisms that are no longer living. Decomposers may return organisms' nutrients to the soil. That helps some food chains start over again since many plants need the nutrients to grow.

3   Three kinds of consumers are herbivores, carnivores, and omnivores. Herbivores are known as primary consumers since they eat mainly plants. Deer, rabbits, cows, and bees are herbivores. So are African elephants; an elephant may eat hundreds of pounds of plants every day. A herbivore, therefore, can be a small insect or the largest animal on the African continent!

4   Carnivores are animals that mainly eat other animals. Cats, frogs, snakes, and hawks are carnivores. Omnivores are organisms that usually eat both plants and animals. Dogs, pigs, hornets, and chickens are omnivores. So are bears and raccoons. Anyone who has been camping knows that. Bears and raccoons will eat almost anything! Pack food away carefully if those two omnivores are around.

GO ON →

Copyright © McGraw-Hill Education

5   Carnivores and omnivores are often called secondary consumers since they follow the first consumers in a food chain, the herbivores. People usually eat from both plant and animal food groups. That means that most people are omnivores. However, vegetarians are herbivores since they mainly eat plant-based food.

6   Decomposers on a food chain have a vital responsibility during the last step in a food chain. There are numerous types of decomposers. Fungi, for example, may break down fallen tree branches while earthworms eat plant life that has died. Various insects, such as beetles and flies, are decomposers, and bacteria, microscopic organisms, also play an important role as decomposers.

7   Every ecosystem has its own food chains. The next time you walk through your own environment, keep your eyes open. Will you be able to identify the producers, consumers, and decomposers?

GO ON →

Journal Entry for May 15

1   Today I hiked through the lovely woods near my home to investigate our local wildlife. I wanted to learn more about my area's amazing ecosystem. I stopped first at the large pond's edge. There I found a fascinating example of a food chain. A food chain is the path that energy takes from one organism to another in the form of food. The woods' strong, hearty populations provide energy-rich, nourishing food for each other.

2   Algae, a producer in the food chain, floated in the pond collecting sunlight and growing quickly. Mayflies, consumers in a food chain, swarmed around feasting on the algae. Fish, also consumers, grabbed some mayflies to eat as they swam near the pond's surface. Since there were so many fish, many birds clustered around the pond. The birds, such as the beautiful herons I saw, looked ready to catch some fish for their meals. Finally, I know decomposers will break down the birds after they die, returning nutrients to the soil.

3   I also saw plenty of herbivores, consumers that mostly eat plants. The caterpillars and bees in the tall trees were just two examples. The trees also sheltered their share of carnivores, animals that mostly eat other animals. I saw hollows in the trees where owls wait for night. Owls, hungry carnivores, will then feast on rodents and other small mammals. These birds run down their prey, hunting and capturing their victims after the sun sets.

4   I had an interesting visit to my area's woods. Since most people are omnivores—that means we eat both plants and animals—I decided to drop by the café near the woods' entrance. I ordered a salad and sandwich—and wrote this journal entry!

Answer these questions about "Food Chains."

19 **Part A:** What is a main idea of "Food Chains"?

(A) Plants don't get enough sunlight.

(B) Energy obtained from food is passed through organisms.

(C) All environments in our world must be protected.

(D) Living things on a food chain must be helped.

Part B: Which **two** of the following provide details that support the main idea in Part A?

(A) "The answer is simple once you think about it." (Paragraph 1)

(B) "Living things get energy from food." (Paragraph 1)

(C) "The energy in food is passed from one organism to another in a food chain." (Paragraph 1)

(D) "Anyone who has been camping knows that." (Paragraph 4)

(E) "Pack food away carefully if those two omnivores are around." (Paragraph 4)

(F) "The next time you walk through your own environment, keep your eyes open." (Paragraph 7)

GO ON →

20 **Part A:** Which type of organism makes its own food as described in the article?

- (A) decomposer
- (B) primary consumer
- (C) secondary consumer
- (D) producer

Part B: Underline **one** sentence in paragraph 2 that **best** supports the answer to Part A.

> Food chains include producers, consumers, and decomposers. First, green plants are called producers in a food chain because they use the Sun's energy to produce their own food. Then animals consume plants and other animals since they cannot make their own food. Animals are called consumers on a food chain. Finally, decomposers on a food chain break down organisms that are no longer living. Decomposers may return organisms' nutrients to the soil. That helps some food chains start over again since many plants need the nutrients to grow.

GO ON →

Name: _____ Date: _____

21 **Part A:** According to "Food Chains," what is the effect of decomposers returning nutrients to the soil?

(A) Sunlight starts most food chains.

(B) Carnivores can then eat decomposers.

(C) Many plants get nutrients they need.

(D) Then decomposers do not need energy from food.

Part B: Which detail from the article shows the cause that supports the answer in Part A?

(A) ". . . many plants need the nutrients to grow." (Paragraph 2)

(B) ". . . largest animal on the African continent!" (Paragraph 3)

(C) ". . . vegetarians are herbivores. . . ." (Paragraph 5)

(D) ". . . numerous types of decomposers." (Paragraph 6)

GO ON →

Answer these questions about "Journal Entry for May 15."

22 **Part A:** What is the meaning of **run down their prey** as it is used in paragraph 3 of the firsthand account?

(A) keep away from other animals to avoid being consumed

(B) run downhill after animals that will be consumed

(C) animals developing poor health so that they can't be consumed

(D) catch animals that will be consumed

Part B: Which phrase from paragraph 3 helps the reader understand the meaning of **run down their prey**?

(A) "... saw hollows in the trees ..."

(B) "... owls wait for night. ..."

(C) "... capturing their victims ..."

(D) "... after the sun sets."

GO ON →

Grade 4 • End-of-Year Assessment

23 **Part A:** What is a main idea of "Journal Entry for May 15"?

(A) Algae won't grow enough unless there is plenty of water.

(B) Healthy populations supply food for each other.

(C) Most birds will only eat fish.

(D) A café must have salads on its menu.

Part B: Which detail from the entry supports the main idea in Part A?

(A) "The woods' strong, hearty populations provide energy-rich, nourishing food for each other." (Paragraph 1)

(B) "Algae, a producer in the food chain, floated in the pond collecting sunlight and growing quickly." (Paragraph 2)

(C) "The birds, such as the beautiful herons I saw, looked ready to catch some fish for their meals." (Paragraph 2)

(D) "I ordered a salad and sandwich—and wrote this journal entry!" (Paragraph 4)

GO ON →

24 **Part A:** According to "Journal Entry for May 15," what is the effect of large populations of fish in the pond?

(A) The pond's algae stops growing.

(B) Many birds can be found near the pond.

(C) Mayflies stay away from the pond.

(D) Decomposers must break down birds that have died.

Part B: Which detail from paragraph 2 shows the cause that supports the answer in Part A?

(A) "Mayflies, consumers in a food chain, swarmed around feasting on the algae."

(B) "Fish, also consumers, grabbed some mayflies to eat as they swam near the pond's surface"

(C) "Since there were so many fish, many birds clustered around the pond."

(D) "Finally, I know decomposers will break down the birds after they die, returning nutrients to the soil."

GO ON →

Name: _____ Date: _____

Now answer these questions about "Food Chains" and "Journal Entry for May 15."

25 **Part A:** Compare and contrast the information about food chains found in the firsthand account "Journal Entry for May 15" with the information found in the secondhand account "Food Chains." Which statement describes the difference in focus of the texts?

(A) "Journal Entry for May 15" focuses on carnivores while "Food Chains" focuses on herbivores and omnivores.

(B) "Journal Entry for May 15" includes some of the author's personal thoughts while "Food Chains" focuses on facts.

(C) "Journal Entry for May 15" does not include any facts while "Food Chains" skips some important facts.

(D) "Journal Entry for May 15" has a different opinion about consumers than "Food Chains."

Part B: Circle **two** phrases that **best** support your answer in Part A.

	Journal Entry for May 15	**Food Chains**
Paragraph 1	". . . I hiked through the lovely woods. . . ."	"Living things need energy. . . ."
Paragraph 2	". . . a producer in the food chain . . ."	". . . food chains start over. . ."
Paragraph 3	". . . small mammals. . ."	". . . largest animal . . ."
Paragraph 4	". . . most people are omnivores. . . ."	". . . raccoons will eat almost anything!"

GO ON →

26 **Part A:** Based on the article and firsthand account, which statement describes environments with successful food chains?

(A) Carnivores get more energy than they really need.

(B) Every population gets enough energy to survive.

(C) Decomposers in the environment include bacteria.

(D) Many trees are growing in the environment.

Part B: Choose **one** phrase from "Food Chains" and **one** phrase from "Journal Entry for May 15" that **best** support the answer to Part A.

(A) ". . . energy in food is passed from one organism to another. . . ." (Food Chains, Paragraph 1)

(B) "Food chains include producers. . . ." (Food Chains, Paragraph 2)

(C) "Herbivores are known as primary consumers. . . ." (Food Chains, Paragraph 3)

(D) ". . . hearty populations provide energy-rich, nourishing food for each other." (Journal Entry for May 15, Paragraph 1)

(E) "Algae, a producer in the food chain, floated in the pond collecting sunlight. . . ." (Journal Entry for May 15, Paragraph 2)

(F) ". . . hollows in the trees where owls wait for night." (Journal Entry for May 15, Paragraph 3)

Narrative Writing 1 Answer Key

Item	Answer	CCSS	Score
1A	A	RL.4.4, L.4.4a	/2
1B	D	RL.4.4, L.4.4a	
2A	B	RL.4.1, RL.4.3	/2
2B	A	RL.4.1, RL.4.3	
3A	C	RL.4.1, RL.4.2	/2
3B	B	RL.4.1, RL.4.2	
4A	C	RL.4.1, RL.4.3	/2
4B	D	RL.4.1, RL.4.3	
5A	"We need to get ready." and Mama had a list for every occasion.	RL.4.1, RL.4.3	/2
5B	C	RL.4.1, RL.4.3	
6	See below	RL.4.1, RL.4.2, RL.4.3 W.4.3, W.4.4, W.4.8, W.4.9a L.4.1, L.4.2, L.4.3, L.4.6	/3 [R] /9 [W] /4 [L]
Total Score			**/26**

6 A top response will include a narrative story with the following key points:

- Carla and her family find a solution to the problems caused by the storm.
- The story ends in a reasonable way that is consistent with the descriptions of plot events and characters found in the beginning of the story.

Narrative Writing 2 Answer Key

Item	Answer	CCSS	Score
1A	C	RI.4.4, L.4.4a	/2
1B	B	RI.4.4, L.4.4a	
2A	B	RI.4.1, RI.4.3	/2
2B	B	RI.4.1, RI.4.3	
3A	C	RI.4.1, RI.4.8	/2
3B	A	RI.4.1, RI.4.8	
4A	A	RI.4.1, RI.4.5	/2
4B	D	RI.4.1, RI.4.5	
5	The following sentences should be selected. "Anyone can enter the competition." "There are also amateur divisions for kids, families, and other people with little or no sculpting experience."	RI.4.1, RI.4.2	/2
6	See below	RI.4.1, RI.4.3 W.4.3, W.4.4, W.4.8, W.4.9 L.4.1, L.4.2, L.4.3, L.4.6	/3 [R] /9 [W] /4 [L]
Total Score			**/26**

6 A top response will include the following key points:

- People of any age can enter the competition, including family teams.
- There are several activities available for both viewing and competition.
- The setting of a beach with lovely sand is enjoyable and fun for all.
- The narrative uses details from the article and includes techniques that make the description compelling and illustrative of the creative and enjoyable scene at the competition.

Literary Analysis 1 Answer Key

Item	Answer	CCSS	Score
1A	C	RL.4.4, L.4.4a	/2
1B	"the broad sweep of flat country that reached to the edge of the sky in all directions"	RL.4.4, L.4.4a	
2A	D	RL.4.1, RL.4.3	/2
2B	C, D	RL.4.1, RL.4.3	
3A	C	RL.4.1, RL.4.2	/2
3B	A	RL.4.1, RL.4.2	
4A	B	RL.4.4, L.4.4a	/2
4B	sunrise – red, red joy morning – smouldering fire noon – golden horns	RL.4.4, L.4.4a, L.4.5a	
5A	C	RL.4.1, RL.4.5, L.4.5a	/2
5B	A	RL.4.1, RL.4.5	
6A	D	RL.4.1, RL.4.3, RL.4.5	/2
6B	B, F	RL.4.1, RL.4.2	
7	See below	RL.4.1, RL.4.3, RL.4.5 W.4.2, W.4.4, W.4.8, W.4.9 L.4.1, L.4.2, L.4.3, L.4.6	/3 [R] /9 [W] /4 [L]
Total Score			**/28**

7 A top response will include a discussion of the following key points:

- Both texts use color words to connect their settings and characters.

- In the passage from *The Wizard of Oz*, the author uses "gray" to describe the dusty, dreary prairie. "Gray" also describes the way Aunt Em and Uncle Henry have grown to look and act like their surroundings. Toto is an active, playful dog with silky black hair and twinkling black eyes. Toto keeps Dorothy cheerful and saves her from becoming as gray as everything that surrounds her.

- "An Indian Summer Day on the Prairie" uses color as a metaphor to describe how the prairie changes from sunrise to sunset. The poet also uses the sun as a character to compare these changes to the changes a person experiences while moving from childhood to old age.

Literary Analysis 2 Answer Key

Item	Answer	CCSS	Score
1	The following details should be included: ". . . something I caught, just like a cold . . ." "'. . . worried I'll never recover.'" ". . . afraid that the 'illness' she'd caught would never heal."	RL.4.4, L.4.4a	/2
2A	A	RL.4.1, RL.4.3	/2
2B	D	RL.4.1, RL.4.3	
3A	B	RL.4.1, RL.4.2	/2
3B	C	RL.4.1, RL.4.2	
4A	C	RL.4.4, L.4.4a	/2
4B	B, D	RL.4.4, L.4.4a	
5	The boxes should have the following details: **Elements of Poetry** • The words at the ends of the lines rhyme. • Each line has the same rhythm. • The two lines are part of a stanza. **Elements of Both Poetry and Prose** • The lines are spoken by a character. • Each line talks about a color. • Both lines are about a type of flower.	RL.4.1, RL.4.5	/2
6A	D	RL.4.1, RL.4.2	/2
6B	A	RL.4.1, RL.4.2	
7	See below	RL.4.1, RL.4.2, RL.4.9 W.4.4, W.4.8, W.4.9 L.4.1, L.4.2, L.4.3, L.4.6	/3 [R] /9 [W] /4 [L]
Total Score			**/28**

7 A top response will include the following key points:

• Both passages have the theme that even when things seem bleak, dark, or disappointing, there is always a positive side, an advantage, or something to look forward to.

• "Life After the Epidemic" is about events that people can sometimes control. For Sandra, finding a positive side to disappointment means looking at those events in a different way. Also, it is a person—John—who helps to point out the positive.

• "The Bluebird's Song" is about the beauty of nature and its patterns. Even when it is dark and wintry outside, there are always flowers ready to grow under the snow. In this text, it is an animal's pure joy—the song of the bluebird—that helps to bring out the positive.

Research Simulation Answer Key

Item	Answer	CCSS	Score
1A	B	RI.4.1, RI.4.4, L.4.4a	/2
1B	C	RI.4.1, RI.4.4, L.4.5c	
2	The following details should be included: **Main Idea:** Neptune balls are a helpful, useful material. **Detail 1:** Neptune balls keep heat from escaping. **Detail 2:** Neptune balls do not rot or grow mold. **Detail 3:** Neptune balls do not catch on fire. **Detail 4:** Neptune balls are easily found in nature.	RI.4.1, RI.4.5	/2
3A	A	RI.4.1, RI.4.8	/2
3B	D	RI.4.1, RI.4.8	
4	See below	RI.4.1, RI.4.2 W.4.2, W.4.4, W.4.7, W.4.8, W.4.9a L.4.1, L.4.2, L.4.3, L.4.6	/3 [R] /9 [W] /4 [L]
5A	D	RI.4.4, L.4.4a	/2
5B	C	RI.4.4, L.4.4a	
6A	B	RI.4.1, RI.4.3	/2
6B	B	RI.4.1, RI.4.3	
7	1: D; 2: C; 3: E; 4: B; 5: A	RI.4.1, RI.4.2	/2
8	See below	RI.4.1, RI.4.3, RI.4.9 W.4.2, W.4.4, W.4.7, W.4.8, W.4.9a L.4.1, L.4.2, L.4.3, L.4.6	/3 [R] /9 [W] /4 [L]
Total Score			**/44**

4 A top response will include the following key points:

- The article's main idea is that two of the future's most useful materials might come from unexpected places—Neptune balls and spider silk.
- Neptune balls may just be balls of seaweed, but they are useful, cheap, resistant to fire, easily found, and environmentally friendly.
- Spider silk may be hard to gather in large amounts, but it is very strong, lightweight, and flexible.
- The essay will include text evidence to support all points.

8 A top response will include the following key points:

- The essay will accurately describe, compare, and contrast the sources and uses of two or three of the following materials: Neptune balls, spider silk, and concrete.
- The essay will include text evidence to support all points.

Narrative 1 Answer Key

Item	Answer	Claim #, Target #	CCSS	DOK	Difficulty	Score
1	A	Claim 1, Target 5				/1
2	See below	Claim 4, Target 2	W.4.2d, W.4.3a, W.4.3c, W.4.3d, W.4.4, W.4.5, W.4.6, W.4.7, W.4.8, W.4.9 L.4.1, L.4.2, L.4.3a, L.4.3b, L.4.6 SL.4.1, SL.4.2, SL.4.3, SL.4.4	4	Medium	/2
3	See below	Claim 4, Target 4				/2
Narrative	See below	Claim 2, Target 2 Claim 2, Target 8 Claim 2, Target 9				/4 [P/O] /4 [D/E] /2 [C]
Total Score						**/15**

2 Responses should include the following key points:

- Both folktales have the following characteristics, as described in the informational article:

  >> They are traditional stories that reflect the customs and beliefs of specific cultures.

  >> They try to teach important lessons about life.

  >> They take on the characteristics of the time and place in which they are told.

  >> They have universal themes.

3 Responses might include the following key points:

- The article provides key characteristics that a folktale should have. These characteristics should be included in an original folktale.

- The two stories are examples of folktales with these key characteristics. They show how the reader can use the characteristics in the article to create a story.

Narrative A top response includes a multi-paragraph original folktale that:

- uses details, dialogue, and description to tell a story that has a beginning, middle, and end

- establishes setting, characters, and a plot consistent with characteristics of a folktale as identified in the source article

- relates ideas to tell a logical sequence of events

- expresses ideas clearly using sensory and/or figurative language as appropriate

- has command of conventions, including punctuation, capitalization, usage, grammar, and spelling

[*See* Narrative Performance Task Scoring Rubric]

Grade 4 • **Performance-Based Tasks Answer Keys**

Narrative 2 Answer Key

Item	Answer	Claim #, Target #	CCSS	DOK	Difficulty	Score
1	See below	Claim 4, Target 2	RI.4.1, RI.4.9 W.4.3a, W.4.3b, W.4.3c, W.4.3d, W.4.3e, W.4.4, W.4.5, W.4.8, W.4.9 L.4.1, L.4.2, L.4.3a, L.4.3b, L.4.6	4	Medium	/2
2	D	Claim 4, Target 12				/1
3	See below	Claim 4, Target 3				/2
Narrative	See below	Claim 2, Target 2 Claim 2, Target 8 Claim 2, Target 9				/4 [P/O] /4 [D/E] /2 [C]
Total Score						**/15**

1 Responses should include the following key points:

- The White House: Our President's Home:

  » provides details about where the President works and lives, including the residence, West Wing, and East Wing of the White House

  » provides details about the floors of the White House

  » provides details about the Oval Office

- Being President:

  » provides details about the activities that the President takes part in on a daily basis, such as reports, meetings, and speeches

3 Responses might include the following key points:

- "Being President" helps to show that the President has a very different job.
- It describes the President's daily activities and explains how these activities are different from everyone else's.
- It shows how the President gives speeches and press conferences, meets world leaders, and must be ready to travel at any moment.

Narrative A top response includes a multi-paragraph narrative that:

- tells about a day in the life of the U.S. President
- is written from the point of view of the President
- uses details and description to tell a story that has a beginning, middle, and end
- establishes setting, characters, and a plot consistent with details identified in the sources
- relates ideas to tell a logical sequence of events
- expresses ideas clearly using sensory and/or figurative language as appropriate
- has command of conventions, including punctuation, capitalization, usage, grammar, and spelling

[See Narrative Performance Task Scoring Rubric]

Opinion 1 Answer Key

Item	Answer	Claim #, Target #	CCSS	DOK	Difficulty	Score
1	B	Claim 4, Target 3	RI.4.1, RI.4.9 W.4.1a, W.4.1b, W.4.1c, W.4.1d, W.4.2d, W.4.3d, W.4.4, W.4.5, W.4.8, W.4.9 L.4.1, L.4.2, L.4.3a, L.4.3b, L.4.6	4	Medium/ High	/1
2	See below	Claim 4, Target 2				/2
3	See below	Claim 4, Target 4				/2
Article	See below	Claim 2, Target 7 Claim 2, Target 8 Claim 2, Target 9				/4 [P/O] /4 [E/E] /2 [C]
Total Score						**/15**

2 Responses might include the following key points and should correctly identify the sources:

- Advantages of bike sharing (one of the following):
    - » Reduces traffic
    - » Convenient
    - » Cheap
    - » Great exercise
    - » Creates jobs
- Disadvantages of bike sharing (one of the following):
    - » Has functionality/logistical problems
    - » Takes up too much space
    - » Can pose a danger or hazard for pedestrians

3 Responses might include the following key points:

- People have difficulty agreeing about bike sharing because there are many good reasons why it is a success, but there are also a lot of valid negative aspects to the programs.
- Students should include at least two supporting details from the sources.

Article A top response includes a multi-paragraph opinion article that:

- clearly gives an opinion about whether their community should start a bike sharing program
- uses details from the sources to support the opinion
- is well-organized and stays on the topic
- uses clear language to express ideas effectively
- has command of conventions, including punctuation, capitalization, usage, grammar, and spelling

[*See* Opinion Performance Task Scoring Rubric]

Opinion 2 Answer Key

Item	Answer	Claim #, Target #	CCSS	DOK	Difficulty	Score
1	C	Claim 4, Target 2	RI.4.1, RI.4.9 W.4.1a, W.4.1b, W.4.1c, W.4.1d, W.4.2d, W.4.3d, W.4.4, W.4.5, W.4.8, W.4.9 L.4.1, L.4.2, L.4.3a, L.4.3b, L.4.6	4	Medium/ High	/1
2	See below	Claim 4, Target 2				/2
3	See below	Claim 4, Target 4				/2
Article	See below	Claim 2, Target 7 Claim 2, Target 8 Claim 2, Target 9				/4 [P/O] /4 [E/E] /2 [C]
Total Score						**/15**

2 Responses should include the following key points:

- The author includes questions to get the reader to think about the problems related to requiring good grades to play a sport after school.
- The questions point out the problems with requiring good grades and how students feel punished by this system.

3 Responses should include the following key points:

- Student should choose one of the opinion articles as providing better support and describe why. Two supporting details should be included from the source, including possibly:

  » Grades Come First!:

    » Schools were not created to train athletes.
    » Allowing students to play without having good grades incorrectly suggests that schoolwork is not important.
    » After-school sports should be viewed as a reward.

  » Sports Are Separate from School:

    » Sports can improve grades.
    » Sports are good for kids mentally and physically.
    » Students learn in different ways.
    » Students should not feel punished if they do not get good grades.
    » Students and their families should decide if they play sports, not the school.

Article A top response includes a multi-paragraph opinion article that:

- clearly gives an opinion about whether good grades should be required to play sports after school
- uses details from the sources to support the opinion
- is well-organized and stays on the topic
- uses clear language to express ideas effectively
- has command of conventions, including punctuation, capitalization, usage, grammar, and spelling

[*See* Opinion Performance Task Scoring Rubric]

Informational Answer Key

Item	Answer	Claim #, Target #	CCSS	DOK	Difficulty	Score
1	B	Claim 4, Target 2	RI.4.1, RI.4.9 W.4.1a, W.4.1b, W.4.2a, W.4.2b, W.4.2c, W.4.2d, W.4.2e, W.4.4, W.4.5, W.4.8, W.4.9 L.4.1, L.4.2, L.4.3	4	Medium/ High	/1
2	See below	Claim 4, Target 2				/2
3	See below	Claim 4, Target 4				/2
Article	See below	Claim 2, Target 4 Claim 2, Target 8 Claim 2, Target 9				/4 [P/O] /4 [E/E] /2 [C]
Total Score						**/15**

2 Responses should include the following key points:

- Just Stand There and Sing:

  >> Ella was cheered on when she sang at the Apollo.

  >> Her song "A-Tisket, A-Tasket" became a number-one hit.

  >> She recorded hundreds of albums, toured around the world, and went on many television shows.

  >> She was the top female jazz singer in the United States for more than 50 years.

  >> She won 13 Grammy Awards and sold 40 million albums.

- Ella Lives On:

  >> She had the nickname the "First Lady of Song."

  >> A group of well-known singers made the disc *We All Love Ella*.

3 Responses might include the following key points:

- Students should choose the second source, "Ella Lives On," and list three of the following pieces of evidence:

  >> People still listen to her today, and she continues to gain new jazz fans.

  >> Countless singers consider her a hero.

  >> A theater was opened in her name, and it holds an annual festival to honor her.

  >> The USPS created a stamp with her face on it.

  >> In 2007 some well-known singers released a disc called *We All Love Ella*.

Article A top response includes a multi-paragraph informational article that:

- clearly describes how Ella Fitzgerald is important to the history of jazz
- uses details from the sources to support the main idea
- is well-organized and stays on the topic
- uses clear language to develop ideas fully
- has command of conventions, including punctuation, capitalization, usage, grammar, and spelling

[*See* Informational Performance Task Scoring Rubric]

End-of-Year Assessment Answer Key

Item	Answer	CCSS	Score
1A	A	RL.4.4, L.4.4a	
1B	First: Has a snack Second: Plays with friends Third: Helps with the dishes	RL.4.1, RL.4.3 L.4.4a, L.4.5	/2
2A	C	RL.4.1, RL.4.2	
2B	"Rita and Ruthie were twin sisters, but their approach to planning their days was completely different."	RL.4.1, RL.4.2, RL.4.3	/2
3A	C	RL.4.1, RL.4.3	
3B	B	RL.4.1, RL.4.3	/2
4A	D	RL.4.1, RL.4.3	
4B	A, B	RL.4.1, RL.4.3	/2
5A	B	RL.4.1, RL.4.3	
5B	D	RL.4.1, RL.4.3	/2
6A	C	RL.4.4, L.4.4a	
6B	D	RL.4.4, L.4.4a	/2
7A	C	RL.4.1, RL.4.3	
7B	C, F	RL.4.1, RL.4.3	/2
8A	B	RL.4.1, RL.4.3	
8B	A	RL.4.1, RL.4.3	/2
9A	A	RL.4.1, RL.4.3	
9B	"Weston realized that if he had taken that room, he might have been accused of the crime."	RL.4.1, RL.4.3	/2
10A	C	RL.4.1, RL.4.3	
10B	A	RL.4.1, RL.4.3	/2
11A	B	RL.4.1, RL.4.2	
11B	D	RL.4.1, RL.4.2	/2
12A	C	RL.4.1, RL.4.3	
12B	D	RL.4.1, RL.4.3	/2
13	Order of statements: C, F, A, B, D	RL.4.1, RL.4.2	/2
14A	C	RI.4.4, L.4.4a, L.4.6	
14B	D	RI.4.4, L.4.4a, L.4.6	/2
15A	B	RI.4.1, RI.4.3	
15B	A	RI.4.1, RI.4.3	/2
16A	D	RI.4.1, RI.4.2	
16B	A, E	RI.4.1, RI.4.2	/2
17A	Order of events: D, A, C, B	RI.4.1, RI.4.5	
17B	B, F	RI.4.1, RI.4.5	/2
18A	A	RI.4.1, RI.4.2	
18B	D	RI.4.1, RI.4.2	/2
19A	B	RI.4.1, RI.4.2	
19B	B, C	RI.4.1, RI.4.2	/2

Item	Answer	CCSS	Score
20A	D	RI.4.1, RI.4.3	/2
20B	"First, green plants are called producers in a food chain because they use the Sun's energy to produce their own food."	RI.4.1, RI.4.3	
21A	C	RI.4.1, RI.4.3	/2
21B	A	RI.4.1, RI.4.3	
22A	D	RI.4.4, L.4.4a, L.4.5b, L.4.6	/2
22B	C	RI.4.4, L.4.4a, L.4.5b, L.4.6	
23A	B	RI.4.1, RI.4.2	/2
23B	A	RI.4.1, RI.4.2	
24A	B	RI.4.1, RI.4.3	/2
24B	C	RI.4.1, RI.4.3	
25A	B	RI.4.1, RI.4.6	/2
25B	". . . I hiked through the lovely woods. . . ." and "Living things need energy. . . ."	RI.4.1, RI.4.6	
26A	B	RI.4.1, RI.4.9	/2
26B	A, D	RI.4.1, RI.4.9	
Total Score			/52

Score	READING Comprehension	WRITING Development of Ideas	WRITING Organization	WRITING Clarity	WRITING Language and Conventions
4	[not applicable]	The response addresses the prompt effectively, develops the topic or narrative logically, and is appropriate to the task and audience.	The response is clear and cohesive and has a strong introduction and conclusion.	The response uses language well. It features sensory details, concrete words, transitions, and appropriate vocabulary.	The response shows strong command of standard English conventions with minor errors that do not impact meaning.
3	The response uses text evidence to support an accurate analysis of the text and shows a full understanding of the ideas in the text.	[not applicable]	[not applicable]	[not applicable]	The response shows command of standard English conventions with a few errors that may impact meaning.
2	The response uses text evidence to support a mostly accurate analysis of the text and shows a broad understanding of the ideas in the text.	The response addresses the prompt, develops the topic or narrative, and is mostly appropriate to the task and audience.	The response is mostly clear and cohesive and has an introduction and conclusion.	The response includes concrete words, sensory details, transitions, and/or domain-specific vocabulary.	The response shows inconsistent command of standard English conventions with errors that interfere with meaning.
1	The response analyzes the text inaccurately or not at all and shows a limited understanding of the ideas in the text.	The response minimally addresses the prompt, does not develop the topic or narrative logically, and may not be appropriate to the task and audience.	The response is sometimes unclear and lacks a real introduction and conclusion.	The response uses language poorly, with limited details, transitions, and/or domain-specific vocabulary.	The response shows slight command of standard English conventions with numerous errors that interfere with meaning.
0	The response analyzes the text inaccurately or not at all and shows little to no understanding.	The response does not address the prompt.	The response is unclear and incoherent.	The response lacks details, transitions, and/or domain-specific vocabulary.	The response shows little or no command of standard English conventions with consistent errors.

Purpose/Organization

4	3	2	1
Organization fully sustained, clear focus: • an effective, unified plot • effectively establishes setting, develops narrator/characters, and maintains point of view • transitions clarify relationships between and among ideas • logical sequence of events • effective opening and closure for audience and purpose	**Organization adequately sustained, focus generally maintained:** • evident plot, but loose connections • adequately maintains a setting, develops narrator/characters, and/or maintains point of view • adequate use of transitional strategies • adequate sequence of events • adequate opening and closure for audience and purpose	**Organization somewhat sustained, may have an uneven focus:** • inconsistent plot, flaws evident • unevenly maintains a setting, develops narrator and/or characters, and/or maintains point of view • uneven use of transitional strategies, little variety • weak or uneven sequence of events • weak opening and closure	**Organization may be maintained but may have little or no focus:** • little or no discernible plot or may just be a series of events • brief or no attempt to establish a setting, narrator and/or characters, and/or point of view • few or no transitional strategies • little or no organization of an event sequence; extraneous ideas • no opening and/or closure

Development/Elaboration

4	3	2	1
Effective elaboration using details, dialogue, and description: • experiences and events are clearly expressed • effective use of relevant source material • effective use of a variety of narrative techniques • effective use of sensory, concrete, and figurative language	**Adequate elaboration using details, dialogue, and description:** • experiences and events are adequately expressed • adequate use of source material contributes to the narration • adequate use of a variety of narrative techniques • adequate use of sensory, concrete, and figurative language	**Uneven elaboration using partial details, dialogue, and description:** • experiences and events are unevenly expressed • weak use of source material that may be vague, abrupt, or imprecise • narrative techniques are uneven and inconsistent • partial or weak use of sensory, concrete, and figurative language	**Minimal elaboration using few or no details, dialogue, and/or description:** • experiences and events may be vague or confusing • little or no use of source material • minimal or incorrect use of narrative techniques • little or no use of sensory, concrete, and figurative language

Conventions

[not applicable]	2	1	0
[not applicable]	**Adequate command of conventions:** • adequate use of correct punctuation, capitalization, usage, grammar, and spelling • few errors	**Partial command of conventions:** • limited use of correct punctuation, capitalization, usage, grammar, and spelling • some patterns of errors	**Little or no command of conventions:** • infrequent use of correct punctuation, capitalization, usage, grammar, and spelling • systematic patterns of errors

NOTE: For Purpose/Organization and Development/Elaboration, responses that are unintelligible, in a language other than English, off-topic, copied text, or off-purpose should receive a score of **NS** (No Score). However, off-purpose responses should receive a numeric score for Conventions.

Purpose/Organization

	4	**3**	**2**	**1**
Purpose/Organization	Clear and effective organizational structure with sustained, consistent, and purposeful focus: • consistent use of a variety of transitions • logical progression of ideas • effective introduction and conclusion • opinion introduced and communicated clearly within the purpose, audience, and task • opposing opinions are clearly addressed (if applicable)	Evident organizational structure with minor flaws; ideas adequately sustained and generally focused: • adequate use of transitions • adequate progression of ideas • adequate introduction and conclusion • opinion is clear and mostly maintained, though loosely • opinion is adequate within the purpose, audience, and task • alternate and opposing opinions are adequately addressed (if applicable)	Inconsistent organizational structure, with evident flaws and somewhat sustained focus: • inconsistent use of transitions • uneven progression of ideas • introduction or conclusion, if present, may be weak • opinion on the issue may be somewhat unclear or unfocused • alternate and opposing opinions may be confusing or not present (if applicable)	Little or no discernible organizational structure, with ideas related to the opinion but little or no focus: • few or no transitions • frequent extraneous ideas are evident; may be formulaic • introduction and/or conclusion may be missing • opinion may be very brief or drift • opinion may be confusing • alternate and opposing opinions may not be present (if applicable)
Evidence/Elaboration	Convincing support/evidence for the main idea, effective use of sources, facts, and details; precise language: • comprehensive evidence from sources is integrated • relevant, specific references • effective elaborative techniques • appropriate domain-specific vocabulary for purpose, audience	Adequate support/evidence for the main idea with adequate use of sources, facts, and details; general language: • some evidence from sources is integrated • general, imprecise references • adequate elaboration • generally appropriate domain-specific vocabulary for audience and purpose	Uneven support/evidence for the main idea, partial use of sources, facts, and details; simple language: • evidence from sources is weakly integrated, vague, or imprecise • vague, unclear references • weak or uneven elaboration • use of domain-specific vocabulary is uneven or somewhat ineffective for the audience and purpose	Minimal support/evidence for the main idea with little or no use of sources, facts, and details; vague: • source material evidence is minimal, incorrect, or irrelevant • references absent or incorrect • minimal, if any, elaboration • use of domain-specific vocabulary is limited or ineffective for the audience and purpose

Conventions

		2	**1**	**0**
Conventions	[not applicable]	Adequate command of conventions: • adequate use of correct punctuation, capitalization, usage, grammar, and spelling • few errors	Partial command of conventions: • limited use of correct punctuation, capitalization, usage, grammar, and spelling • some patterns of errors	Little or no command of conventions: • infrequent use of correct punctuation, capitalization, usage, grammar, and spelling • systematic patterns of errors

NOTE: For Purpose/Organization and Evidence/Elaboration, responses that are unintelligible, in a language other than English, off-topic, copied text, or off-purpose should receive a score of **NS** (No Score). However, off-purpose responses should receive a numeric score for Conventions.

INFORMATIONAL SCORING RUBRIC

Purpose/Organization

4	3	2	1
Clear organizational structure, purposeful focus: • consistent use of a variety of transitions • logical progression of ideas • main idea stated clearly based on purpose, audience, and task	Evident organizational structure, general focus: • adequate, somewhat varied use of transitions • adequate progression of ideas • adequate statement of main idea based on purpose, audience, and task	Inconsistent organizational structure, somewhat focused: • inconsistent use of transitions and/or little variety • uneven progression of ideas; formulaic • main idea may be unclear and/or somewhat unfocused	Little or no organizational structure or focus: • few or no transitions • frequent extraneous ideas; may be formulaic • may lack introduction and/or conclusion • may be very brief, with confusing or ambiguous focus

Evidence/Elaboration

4	3	2	1
Thorough and convincing support for main idea; effective use of sources, facts, and details: • integrates comprehensive evidence from sources • relevant references • effective use of elaboration • domain-specific vocabulary is clearly appropriate for audience and purpose	Adequate support for main idea; uses sources, facts, and details: • some integration of evidence from sources • references may be general • adequate use of some elaboration • domain-specific vocabulary is generally appropriate for audience and purpose	Uneven, cursory support for main idea; uneven or limited use of sources, facts, and details: • weakly integrated, vague, or imprecise evidence from sources • references are vague or absent • weak or uneven elaboration • domain-specific vocabulary is uneven or somewhat ineffective for audience and purpose	Minimal support for main idea; little or no use of sources, facts, and details: • minimal, absent, incorrect, or irrelevant evidence from sources • references are absent or incorrect • minimal, if any, elaboration • domain-specific vocabulary is limited or ineffective for audience and purpose

Conventions

[not applicable]	2	1	0
	Adequate command of conventions: • adequate use of correct punctuation, capitalization, usage, grammar, and spelling • few errors	Partial command of conventions: • limited use of correct punctuation, capitalization, usage, grammar, and spelling • some patterns of errors	Little or no command of conventions: • infrequent use of correct punctuation, capitalization, usage, grammar, and spelling • systematic patterns of errors

NOTE: For Purpose/Organization and Evidence/Elaboration, responses that are unintelligible, in a language other than English, off-topic, copied text, or off-purpose should receive a score of **NS** (No Score). However, off-purpose responses should receive a numeric score for Conventions.